The Questions of Jesus

By
William S. Deal, M.A., Th.D.

The Most Important Questions Which Christ
Asked in the Four Gospels, With Answers
Applied to Modern Day Christian Living.

ISBN 0-88019-294-1

Printed by
Old Paths Tract Society
Shoals, IN 47581

In Honor of Dr. William S. Deal

THE QUESTIONS OF JESUS is one of the very last manuscripts written by Dr. William S. Deal before his elevation to Heaven. This book of "QUESTIONS," with its answers, is especially good for the earnest seeker after the mind and will of God for his daily life.

In this last book, Dr. Deal uses his many skills to make God's Word indelibly clear. Because of the nature and scope of QUESTIONS OF JESUS, his unique ability to focus on God's truth is given full play.

Dr. William S. Deal was a unique and gifted man and wielded a great and godly influence in the Holiness Movement around the world. His writings and preaching were clear and pungent. They exalted Jesus Christ and made the way of holiness practical.

Along with the many other volumes written by Dr. Deal, I commend this book to the praying seeker after Biblical truths. His voice is silent, but his books minister to young and old.

Contents

	PAGE
Preface	7
1. A Question of Duty	9
2. A Question of Seeking	11
3. A Question of Believing	13
4. A Question of Exchange	15
5. A Question of Concern	17
6. A Question of How	19
7. A Question of Separation	21
8. A Question of Ceremony	23
9. A Question of Fear	25
10. A Question of Right	27
11. A Question of Proper Conduct	29
12. A Question of Bread	31
13. A Question of Preserving	33
14. A Question of a Name	35
15. A Question of Reading	37
16. A Question of Healing	39
17. A Question of Discernment	42
18. A Question of Fragments	44
19. A Question of Faith	47
20. A Question of Murder	49
21. A Question of Accusers	51
22. A Question of Kindred	53
23. A Question of Who Is My Neighbor	55
24. A Question of God's Giving	58
25. A Question of Consequences	60
26. A Question of Commitment	62
27. A Question of Ownership	64
28. A Question of Ability	67
29. A Question of Going	69

30. A Question of Knowing 71
31. A Question of Willingness 73
32. A Question of Perplexity 75
33. A Question of Desire 77
34. A Question of Husbandry 79
35. A Question of Numbers 81
36. A Question of Acquaintance 83
37. A Question of Faithfulness 85
38. A Question of Trouble 87
39. A Question of Lacking 89
40. A Question of Escape 91
41. A Question of Inquisitiveness 93
42. A Question of Finding 96
43. A Question of Weeping 98
44. A Question of Suffering 100
45. A Question of Watching 102
46. A Question of Seeing 104
47. A Question of Execution 106
48. A Question of Touch 108
49. A Question of Purpose 109
50. A Question of Impiety 111
51. A Question of Likeness 113
52. A Question of Knowledge 114
53. A Question of Words 116
54. A Question of Reward 117
55. A Question of Dividing 119
56. A Question of the Times 120
57. A Question of Understanding 121
58. A Question of Signs 123
59. A Question of What To Say 124
60. A Question of Intention 126
61. A Question of Placing 128
62. A Question of Supposition 130
63. A Question of Sufficiency 132
64. A Question of Images 134
65. A Question of Comparison 136
66. A Question of Smiting 138

Author's Preface

This book came about in the following manner: Someone had listed in a minister's magazine all the questions which Christ asked in the Gospels with their references. The list was not signed, and therefore, remains anonymous. As soon as I read the list, I was deeply impressed that here was material for a good and useful book. After about a year's work, here is that book!

The major questions of Christ, as recorded in the Gospels, are covered in this book. Each question presented has been thoroughly examined; the proper historical, and often geographical, settings have been given; all major Greek words used in such questions have been examined and explained. A *practical* application to daily Christian living has been made where possible, as well as a critical analysis for the subject given.

Ministers, Sunday school teachers, youth leaders, camp and Bible conference workers, as well as all laymen, will be deeply interested in this work. It offers the results of much painstaking labor to present the kernels of truth which cluster about these forever famous questions. As far as is known, no other book of this kind is in circulation today.

The simplicity and directness of approach in this book will, we hope, be appealing. It is hoped that readers will pass it along to their friends. May God add His blessing to its messages of hope, love and spiritual power.

—William S. Deal

QUESTION 1

A Question of Duty

"How is it that ye sought me? Wist ye not that I must be about my Father's business?" Luke 2:49.

In presenting the questions of Christ, it seems appropriate that we should begin with His first recorded question in the New Testament.

Jewish boys were to be presented to God at twelve years of age. After proper instruction at this time, they became "sons of the Law." Joseph and Mary had taken Jesus to Jerusalem for this purpose. After these ceremonies, they visited with relatives and friends, but Jesus busied Himself with the doctors of the law, asking and answering questions. He was concerned about His life's work and wanted to secure all possible information about it.

Although Jesus was the Son of God, He experienced a growth in the knowledge of God as well as in His humanity. He "increased in wisdom and stature, and in favour with God and man" (Luke 2:52). One of the mysteries of the incarnation is how the deity of Christ could remain in Him, unimpaired, and yet He could "increase in favour with God." As Jesus was perfect man, as well as God, this increase in wisdom indicates His growth in human awareness of His deity as His rational soul grew in its apprehensions of life. The astonishment of the doctors of the law at His wisdom and answers indicates with what rapid progress this knowledge had been unfolded to His.

When Joseph and Mary found Him in the temple and asked, "Son, why hast thou thus dealt with us?" they were hardly prepared for His questions at the head of this chapter. The word "business" in this quotation may better be rendered *concern*. To paraphrase it, He asked them, "Why did you not look in the temple first? Do you not understand that I am interested in what concerns My Father?"

This burning question must have brought to their minds things of years ago, when angels announced His birth and mission. Had they taken Him too much for granted? Had His constant presence with them dulled their apprehension of His mission, How easily the heart is dulled about divine things by earthly surroundings!

The divine awareness in Jesus at this tender age was great. But has it not been manifested to others in tender youth, such as Samuel and David? About this age there often occurs a great awakening of God's dealings with youth. Pity the parents who do not see this and direct their children properly in their response to it.

Jesus' returning to Nazareth and becoming subject to Joseph and Mary does not indicate that He failed to carry out His Father's will. This was part of that mission and of the preparation for His coming ministry. Youth must understand that growth, development and training are essential to successful life. Youth are serving God just as much during this period as when on some special field of mission in later years.

The "silent years" of Jesus—from twelve to thirty—were an essential part of the preparation for His life's work and redemptive mission. His work in carpentry was evidenced by the clamor of the public (Matt. 13:55) when He was in His public ministry. They could hardly believe He could have become so profound a speaker and teacher. But these very years as a working man forever dignified labor and fitted Him, humanly, to understand and have compassion upon the laboring, the weary and the poor. He was among the most poor (Matt. 13:54-56) and consequently, in His public ministry, was filled with conpassion, tenderness, wisdom and love, and an unrivaled understanding of mankind and his needs.

Jesus Christ still says to youth today, "Do you not understand that you should be interested in what concerns your Father?" He is calling all youth today to a life of usefulness and service to God and humanity.

QUESTION 2

A Question of Seeking

"What seek ye?" John 1:38.

Jesus had just been baptized by John and was now entering upon His public ministry. When Jesus was aware that some of John's disciples had started to follow Him, He asked them, "What seek ye?" They asked where He dwelt, and He invited them to "come and see."

Christ did not promise these men anything; He merely invited them to share His fare with Him. One of these men was Andrew. He won to Christ his brother, Simon, who became the mighty Apostle Peter.

Christ here introduces another of life's great questions. To paraphrase, *"What do you seek in life? What do you want of Me?"* He probes motives to the depths. He asks, "What are your motives for life? Why are you following Me? Are you following Me merely for the good you can get from it?"

Men's motives for identifying themselves with any cause are of the utmost importance. Right motives guide us to put our best into anything in life. Selfish motives make our services of little value. The same is true in our relationship to Christ and His church. If we claim fellowship with Christ but are always reluctant to render any worthwhile service to His cause, it is evident that our purpose in belonging to His church is more selfish than pure.

The great southern Methodist evangelist, Sam P. Jones, exclaimed, "Most Christians are hell-scared Christians!" Too many have accepted Christ as a "fire escape from hell," instead of out of pure love for God and appreciation of Christ's redemptive work. The supreme motive for serving God should be our devotion to Him and love for His cause.

Examine your motives. Ask yourself candidly, "What is my purpose in what I am seeking to do or to gain? Can I truthfully say I am seeking this in the light of the words which say, 'All that ye do, therefore, whether ye eat or drink, do all to the glory of God'?"

Two other questions of Christ's are on this same line. When they came to arrest Him He asked, "Whom seek ye?" Of Mary, on the resurrection morning, He asked, "Whom seekest thou?" (John 18:4, 20:15).

Here the question is not of *what*, but of *whom*. Our motives may be probed even deeper. Do we seek the highest goal in life? Are our goals always only those the Saviour would approve? Have we placed all others aside and put Him first in all our life's seekings and strivings? Is it our deepest desire and highest ambition to please Him in all our undertakings?

The "whats" of our lives may be materialistic, earthly, and physical; but the "whoms" of life are far more penetratingly spiritual. With whom do we identify ourselves most? With Christ and His followers, or with those who have no love for Him or any concern for His work?

QUESTION 3

A Question of Believing

"Believest thou?" John 1:50.

Jesus had only recently been baptized by John and had just started His ministry when He was introduced to Nathanael. As he approached, Jesus said to him, "Behold an Israelite indeed, in whom is no guile." Astounded, Nathanael wondered how He knew him. Christ told him He had seen Him "under the fig tree"—a statement which caused Nathanael to exclaim that Jesus was the Son of God. Then Jesus asked, "Because I said unto thee, I saw thee under the fig tree, believest thou? thou shalt see greater things than these."

Christ's ability to read Nathanael's heart-life must have been one of the great factors of convincing him that Christ was the Son of God. Christ's pronouncement convinced him that Jesus had supernatural power, and made him certain that he was face to face with deity.

At this early time in Christ's ministry He had already been proclaimed "the Lamb of God" by John the Baptist, and "the Messiah" by another of His followers. Now, Nathanael calls Him "the Son of God." In none of these cases does Christ deny these claims—a thing which He *must necessarily* have done to be true to His moral code had He *not been* truly these things.

It is not likely that Nathanael understood fully the meaning of the term "Son of God" as we do today. He may not have understood all about Christ's redemptive mission and the extent of His great work. But after all the Christian centuries, how many sinners today, meeting Christ for the first time in real eye-opening conviction, realize the fullness of His mission and work? Yet, their faith in Him as Son of God is unshaken. The early disciples had no complete understanding of the unique person and Great work of Christ, but this did not hinder their faith in Him from shining out.

When Christ asked, "Believest thou?" He showed what was the heart of true Christianity. It is a religion with faith as its essential keystone. This confidence in Christ by which the Christian *now* accepts Him as Lord and Master, and Saviour-King, is the keystone in the arch of Christianity. Take this faith away, and there is nothing left except noble moralizations, a good code of ethics, and a set of high principles. All these without the spiritual *power* on the part of the follower to put them into action mean nothing of saving grace.

This faith in the Sonship and deity of Christ keeps the believer's heart through Christ's abiding presence and gives life and power to the Christian religion. A professed follower of Christ without this divine life in his heart is like a model car or airplane without a motor—only a cold symbol of the genuine thing!

Across the centuries Christ is still asking of His followers, "Believe ye that I am able to do this?" Only when the heart responds with positive affirmation, bringing a newness of life, a living demonstration of Christian grace, is one truly a real believer.

QUESTION 4

A Question of Exchange

"What shall a man give in exchange for his soul?" Mark 8:37.

Jesus had just reminded His followers of the importance of cross-bearing in the new way of life which He was offering. He had pointed out that to "save" one's life for himself was to "lose" it in the end. His kingdom called for the whole-hearted who had counted the cost and held nothing too dear to sacrifice for His cause.

To "gain the world," He said, was to "lose the soul." As this truth sank down into the hearts of His listeners, He posed the burning question, as if to give them an afterthought, "What shall a man give in exchange for his soul?"

Let the words of this question echo in the heart. Can a man *sell* his soul? Make merchandise of the most valuable thing he possesses? Can one afford to barter his very innermost self for transient, sensual, fleshly pleasures of short duration? It is to be feared that millions are doing something akin to this. They have been so busy with sensual and selfish living that they have bartered their souls for its temporary pleasures, almost without realization. They have exchanged a tender conscience for a hardened one, a loving heart for a deceitful, wicked one, and the noble aspirations and ambitions of youth for a set of sordid principles, evil ambitions and vile intentions.

A famous movie star, speaking of the many opportunities of modern youth in the entertainment world, cried, "I would have *given my soul* for a chance like this when I was young!" Perhaps she had already *given her soul* for her place of success in the world of make-believe!

Who can equate the priceless value of the human soul against all of earth's wealth? If one owned this earth, as a solid ball of purest gold, and every mountain a sparkling diamond, it would not make a down payment on the value of the human soul! If one could reach into the starry heavens and pick out a universal system with all its glory or go to the farthest areas of sidereal space, he could not find enough material wealth in all the undiscovered universes to purchase one immortal *soul*!

Could the lost from yonder's world of endless night and sorrow come back for only one hour and find a place of repentance and restoration to favor with God, they would not exchange it for all the creations of God, terrestrial or celestial. Man does not know the value of his own soul.

QUESTION 5

A Question of Concern

"Woman, what have I to do with thee?" John 2:4.

Jesus and His disciples attended a wedding in Cana of Galilee. Jesus' mother seems to have been in charge of the entertainment. Attendance was greater than anticipated and there was a shortage of the drink being served.

Mary turned to Jesus and mentioned this situation. Perhaps it was embarrassing to her and the others in charge of entertainment. Jesus said simply, "Woman, what have I to do with thee?" Then He reminded her that His time had not yet come.

Mary took the cue. Turning to the servants, she pointed to her Son and said, "Ahatsoever He saith unto you, do it."

Some scholars believe that the bridegroom of this marriage was young John, the future apostle John, who was so close to Christ during His ministry. This was Christ's first miracle in that area. John was just starting out to follow Christ. Jesus was there to show His love and care for him and his new bride. Jesus rescued John from what might have become an embarrassing situation, by providing ample wine for his wedding.

Jesus' question seems to express disassociation from the whole affair on the surface, but such was far from the case. Christ's concern for His young disciple was very deep and thorough. When the circumstances were proper, His power was demonstrated in performing this miracle. Perhaps the servants did not understand His orders at first, just as we often do not understand His workings when we first begin to live for Him.

The clear water poured into the pots was carried to the master of ceremonies in the feasting chamber. He exclaimed,

"Thou hast saved the good wine until now!" This probably indicated its fresh and unfermented state.

How much like the Lord Jesus Christ to come to the rescue of His beloved friend in the hour of greatest need. He never fails.

It must not be thought, however, that this marvelous miracle was done just to rescue John from an embarrassing situation, nor to keep an otherwise happy wedding from becoming a disappointing affair. Such a display of divine power would have been most unworthy of the character of Christ.

The key to the miracle is that it "manifested forth his glory; and his disciples believed on him" (John 2:11). The *occasion*, while important, is not the prime reason for the miracle at all. Just as our healing or deliverance from imperiling situations is never the prime reason for His miracle-working power. Only when good can be for His glory, and our ultimate best does it occur. Sometimes it seems there is such a worthy cause for a miracle or the healing of someone, from *our* viewpoint, but Christ knows that for the most desired miracle to occur, our ultimate best ends would not be served. Therefore, it does not happen.

Christ performs miracles in our lives only when the purposes of His highest glory and our ultimate best good will be served.

QUESTION 6

A Question of How

"If I have told you earthly things, and ye believe not, how shall ye believe, if I tell you of heavenly things?" John 3:12.

Nicodemus came to Jesus for personal information about the kingdom of God. He was a sincere man, as proved by his willingness to accept Christ's explanation and become a follower of His. Nicodemus should have declared himself, but the Word says he was a disciple "secretly, for fear of the Jews."

During this famous interview Jesus explained the "new birth," and stated positively its necessity. He told Nicodemus that to enter into the kingdom of God, he must "be born from above," as a better rendering from the Greek should be.

This strange, supernatural experience, by which one becomes a child of God, brings God's forgiveness of sins when the person repents and reconciliation to God through Christ. It is witnessed to by one's own consciousness that he has met God's demands for salvation and by the Holy Spirit in his innermost consciousness, that this work is done (Rom. 8:16).

This gracious work of God is known in the Scripture as *justification*—the legal act of God in releasing the person from all guilt through Christ; and as *regeneration*—the moral act of God by which man becomes a partaker of the divine life of God, imparted by grace into the soul.

Jesus explained this to Nicodemus in non-technical terms, but Nicodemus did not understand. He wanted to know how he could be born again.

Jesus patiently explained to him that it was a *spiritual*, not a physical, matter. Christ was disappointed at Nicodemus, being a "ruler of the Jews," yet having such spiritual density. He asked Nicodemus, "If I have told you earthly things, and ye believe not, how shall ye believe, if I tell you of heavenly things?"

This proved a stinging question. Nicodemus asked nothing more. Christ then explained God's provision for salvation, climaxing this masterful address with John 3:21.

Perhaps the best known passage in the Bible is John 3:16. It was not spoken to a hugh multitude where the rapport of the crowd would have brought back a most hearty acceptance. Rather, it was spoken to one lone listener, hungering to know more of the way of God. This exhibits Christ's personal touch and interest in all of us.

There is a sigh in the Saviour's voice in this question. To paraphrase it, "Oh, Nicodemus, if you cannot understand human truth, how can you grasp divine things?"

The "how" of spiritual things is not easily understood by the unconverted. But if one will throw himself on the mercy of God, he will come to know the joy of redeeming love.

QUESTION 7

A Question of Separation

"Will ye also go away?" John 6:67.

Jesus had just laid down the highest principles of His kingdom. He had told the people that if they were to follow Him, they must get past the idea of following for "the loaves and fishes." To come into a spiritual relationship with Him, He explained, they must "eat" His flesh and "drink" His blood.

This was indeed a "hard saying." Many complained that they did not understand what was meant, but rather than confess their ignorance and ask His meaning, they only murmured their complaints.

Some people when traveling simply *will not* break down and ask for directions until they have lost time, driven out of their way, and exhausted a lot of patience. Usually, they end up asking someone at last. Why not admit ignorance, ask at *first* and save time, money and energy, foolishly spent trying to "save face"?

Man wants to make his own way. He wishes to impress others with his wisdom, prudence, and power of prowess, thereby *making* his own *mark* in the world. Most men have made their mark, as someone aptly put it—generally, a *long, black, crooked* one!

Had the people but asked, He would have told them that to *eat His flesh* is only to *feed the soul upon His Word,* and to *drink His blood* is but to *be filled and guided by His Holy Spirit.* Christ explained, "He that eateth my flesh and drinketh my blood, dwelleth in me, and I in him" (John 6:56). He spoke not of the physical flesh, but of the spiritual nature.

When the crowd walked away in apparent disgust, Christ turned to His apostles and asked, "Will ye also go away?" (John

6:67). Peter replied instantly, "Lord, to whom shall we go? thou hast the words of eternal life. And we believe and are sure that thou art that Christ, the Son of the living God" (John 6:68, 69).

What a burning question, "Will ye also go away?" Will you also separate yourselves from the only Source of light and life, truth and grace; forgiveness, cleansing, happiness and eternal good? From that time, "many of his disciples went back, and walked no more with him" (John 6:66). What a tragic note! How sad must those poor disillusioned souls be today, living on in eternal darkness, somewhere far beyond the bounds of God's mercy and His love.

QUESTION 8

A Question of Ceremony

"Why make ye this ado, and weep?" Mark 5:39.

Jairus, a ruler of one of the local synagogues, came to Christ with a perplexing problem. His daughter was seriously ill; would Jesus come and heal her? Christ answered affirmatively and set out in that direction. But as He traveled He was thronged by needy people and stopped to administer to these. Jairus' heart must have ached, hoping He *would hurry on* before it was too late!

How often have our hearts, too, been longing, praying and even *urging* the Master to meet some need of ours at once. And how many times He has delayed His coming.

Whether Christ comes now or later; whether He solves our problem as we see the need or in another way, is of little consequence. It is sufficient to know that He has it in hand and is working it out in the way that is best.

Our prayers, too, are in the mind of God, and He begins to work for us from the moment of their utterance. But there are reasons why He sometimes delays the answer, just as there were in Jairus' case.

A messenger came saying, "Why trouble the Master any further? Thy daughter is dead." But the man could not take "no" for an answer. Jesus said, "Be not afraid, only believe." To paraphrase it, "Don't worry; I have your case in My hands, and I will take care of it." What more could one want? Oh, troubled soul, awaiting an answer to prayer, rest assured, the Master has the situation in hand.

As Christ stepped into the room where the mourners were, He asked, *"Why make ye this ado, and weep?"* Then He said, "The damsel is not dead, but sleepeth." Then they "laughed him to scorn." They were *paid mourners*, hired to weep over the dead. This is why they could turn so abruptly from mourning to laughing.

Here is dead "ceremony" with no power to raise the dead, nor even to truly sympathize with the bereft parents. Once the corpse was entombed, it collected its fees for "mourning" and went its way to play the whole miserable role over again.

Lifeless, cold *ceremony* in religious worship is little more than mockery! Often the heart bleeds for affection, understanding, and sympathy, but, in response, how often cold, dead ceremony perfunctorily goes through the ritual, or mumbles pious words of would-be comfort. Underneath it is a heart dead, cold, and lifeless toward the real need. How many who come expecting to get a refreshing drink for the parching soul are met with merely a bubble of cold air.

Christ put the fake mourners out and, going directly to the bedside of the dead child, gave her life again. This was a scathing condemnation of the cold and heartless. What a shame that those best suited to minister to the needs of broken humanity are too often merely "professional" in their approach to human needs!

QUESTION 9

A Question of Fear

"Why are ye so fearful? how is it that ye have no faith?" Mark 4:40.

Jesus had just preached to a great throng by the shore of Galilee giving them some of His rich parable-stories of truth. He dismissed the crowd and prepared to go to another community to preach, probably the next day.

The disciples used a large fishing boat for the cruise to the other side of the Sea of Galilee. Being weary, Jesus retired to the stern of the boat and soon fell asleep upon a large mat— referred to by Mark as a "pillow." For the first while, the ship moved along smoothly; the night was calm and placid.

The Sea of Galilee often becomes stormy in a hurry. The wind sweeps down from the nearby hills and churns the water into boinsterous, angry waves in a short time.

Howling winds whipped away at the sails of the boat. The waters became boisterous, slopping right over into the boat. Being extra tired, the Master slept through it all. When the waves crested to such heights that Peter and others feared the boat would never ride out the storm, they came to Jesus and awoke Him. Raging waves lashed in maddening fury against the boat as if to upset it. The disciples could contain themselves no longer. Iin dismay they cried out, almost in unison, "Master, carest thou not that we perish?" He must have turned and looked into their anguished eyes, ever so silently, and then asked, "Why are ye so fearful; how is it that ye have no faith?"

How often we paddle our own canoe and face whatever storms come, until they become so fearful we can no longer face them alone. Then, we turn in our helplessness to the Lord. Just as then, He has been nearby all the time. We have only been too self-reliant, stubborn, or shy to ask Him for help. And just as with them, as soon as we turn to Him with all our hearts, we find Him ever ready to aid us.

But what of the questions, "Why are ye so fearful? How is it that ye have no faith?" These questions must have burned in the disciples' hearts. Were they questions of rebuke, of gentle reminder, or of deep heart-hurt, upon the Saviour's part? Was He probing their hearts for faith, or was He bringing them up short for their lack of pressing their own faith into action at this time?

Could they have rebuked the sea and wind in His name and obtained the same calm as He did? This may remain an unanswered question. It is doubtful that they had this faith then, for they had not seen it demonstrated before. His rebuke seems rather timed to their fear than to their failure to calm the sea.

Christ does not expect us to do the impossible, nor to take His place in His great work. But He does expect our trust and confidence in Him to dispel our fears when in His presence. How could the disciples have reasoned that He would abandon them in the storm and go walking off on the sea, allowing their boat to flounder and sink? They had no real right to doubt that He would care for them. And yet, it seems that they were almost overcome with fear.

How like the human race! God can prove Himself a thousand times, and yet, many tend to panic again when the next storm arises upon the horizon. How small is our faith! His mercy and kindness are demonstrated in this story, and repeated untold times in our lives. Let us "have faith in God," and lose our fears of life and its changing situations and perplexities.

QUESTION 10

A Question of Right

". . . Is it lawful on the sabbath days to do good, or to do evil? to save life, or to destroy it?" Luke 6:9.

Christ asked this question when He was about to heal the man with the withered hand. The scribes and Pharisees looked on with accusing hearts. Christ was about to put their religion to a supreme test—which was more important, to do good and help someone in need, or to stick strictly to the ceremonial limitations demanded by extreme formalists in their interpretation of the law?

The religious leaders wanted to make Him appear wicked to the public, and destroy His influence. Christ knew their intentions and anticipated them with His burning question. Stunned by it, they stalled for an answer. He then reminded them that they would not leave an innocent sheep or an ox in the ditch to suffer alone on the sabbath. This they could not deny.

Christ proceeded to thunder at them, "How much is a man better than a sheep?" (Matt. 12:12). Asking the crippled man to extend his hand, Christ restored it even as the other hand.

What shouts of praise must have gone up from the healed man and the multitude about him. The people were happy to see the man healed and the cold formalists silenced by a mighty demonstration of divine power.

One would think the leaders would have acknowledged Christ and His divine authority, but they went away "filled with madness," and seeking to "destroy him." Oh, how blind is a religious formalist! He can witness the mightiest displays of divine power, see the miraculous power of Christ change men, before his very eyes, from drunkards and thugs to wholesome Christians, and continue to oppose this display of divine power as if it had never occured. There is nothing harder to pierce than the mail-coat of an armor-plated formalist.

Questions of right and wrong are not always easy to settle. Where there are delicate lines of religious coloration, or where there are old and strong traditions upholding a certain thing, even wrong may become entrenched so strongly and colored so cleverly that it appears as right. Only by the strongest light from God's Word and the power of the Holy Spirit can one so entrenched be made to see differently.

Today, the Lord's day is almost without regard. It is desecrated by millions, seemingly without a compunction of conscience. The masses accept the New Testament freedom that the day is one of worship, not of strict adherence to the Old Testament sabbath. Then they take liberties which largely destroy the purpose of the day.

QUESTION 11

A Question of Proper Conduct

"If ye love them which love you, what thank have ye? for sinners also love those that love them. And if ye lend to them of whom ye hope to receive, what thank have ye? for sinners also lend to sinners, to receive as much again" Luke 6:32, 34.

After choosing His twelve apostles, Jesus explained to them the difference between His gospel of salvation and the old economy of Law. It had said, "An eye for an eye, and a tooth for a tooth." If one put out another's eye, one of his eyes was to be put out in retaliation for his evil deed.

Jesus explained that to merely fulfill the old laws was not sufficient. In doing this He used the illustration in the questions above. Some people's religion goes no farther than the little old lady who said, "They say the Bible says do *good* for *evil;* I won't do it; I'll do *good* for *good,* and that's all I will do!" Anyone can do this, without God's grace in his heart.

Christ is here saying, "You must do no more than love the loving, respond to those who honor you, and do good only to the fellow who gives you a glad hand and a nice compliment."

Do not even heathen return *good* for *good* to their fellows? And indeed, do not some, as Ghandi of India did, even go farther and return good for evil? These are persons who make no profession of grace, who have restrained themselves when mistreated and even gone so far as to return a kind favor for an evil, under-handed deed.

What is there in your religion which will make it stand the testing fires of God's judgment? Will it bear patiently the blows of our cruel society, without retaliatory acts or remarks? Is there anything in it above and beyond the strength and power of endurance, of sheer human patience, and its ability to be kind even when mistreated? If not, then it is no more than the religion of Cain!

Oh, how much religion of our times is honeycombed with mere human politeness, untouched with divine compassion, unanointed with intercessory prayer and knows nothing of a burning desire to win others to Jesus Christ!

The religion of Jesus Christ is not mere external politeness, culture, and refinement. These may be only the by-products of a true Christian experience, whose power and glory in heart have long since passed away. Just as the sunset's afterglow often lingers long in earth's northern highlands, so there are often lingering accessories of a true religious experience long after one has ceased to have an inward consciousness of God.

Jesus explained that the test of genuine religion is not so much its *outward forms* as its *inward heart*. Christianity is not a religion of negatives, but of positives. It is the religion of the heart which causes one to spontaneously love and do good to men. His criterion of it was, "Love your enemies . . . do good to them that despitefully use you . . . lend, hoping for nothing again . . . be merciful to others . . . judge not . . . forgive others . . . give to others . . . and 'ye shall be the children of the Highest. . . .' "

Sam P. Jones once said, "I had rather be in heaven learning my ABC's than sitting in hell reading Greek!" We may be only in the learning stages, but this is far better than success in the world.

QUESTION 12

A Question of Bread

"How many loaves have ye?" Mark 6:33; 8:5.

Jesus had quite a bit to say about bread. He used it both literally and spoke of it symbolically in His life and ministry. "Bread" does not always refer to just the particular item made from flour or meal. Often in Scripture it refers to "food" in general. For instance, in Jesus' words, "Man shall not live by bread alone." Literally, not by *physical food alone.*

In the following passages note the variety of words: "How many loaves have ye?" In Luke 24:41 the word "meat" is used, referring doubtless to bread or food in general; while in John 21:5 the word is also "meat." Verse 9, however, refers to both "fish . . . and bread." Life substance, normal food, is therefore beyond doubt the more literal meaning of the term *bread* in the Scriptures, unless specifically identified as bread alone.

In both passages in Mark *food* seems to be the thought, as both fish and bread were produced in response to His question, which in turn He fed to the multitudes.

There are several valuable suggestions in this question. Bread is the "staff of life." An Old Testament writer put it, "bread . . . to strengthen man's heart." Food is of the highest importance for life, next to air and water. These three elements are absolutely essential to physical survival.

God has mercifully placed these elements in reach of all, and only in exceptions do persons die for want of them. There are unfortunate areas of the earth where most people never have sufficient food, but none where drink and air are not available. Man's sinfulness has cut his limitations of food. The ground does not bring forth as abundantly as it did in Eden, since it, too, was cursed as a result of man's disobedience and sin. Almost without exception, lands where there is a serious food shortage are the lands which have not accepted the Gospel of Christ.

Multiplied millions around the world have felt the Christian pulse of America in the untold billions of dollars given to needy areas. Other unnumbered millions are asking us for what is far more important—the *message* of the *Bread of Life!*

"Have ye any bread?" ought to be a soul-searching question with everyone of us. Christ is the Bread of Life, and we are to *share Him* with the whole world. Jesus commissioned the Church to "Go ye into all the world, and preach the gospel to every creature" (Mark 16:15). How, then, can we delay proclaiming this message to relatives, neighbors and the world? If their eternal welfare hinges upon their acceptance of Him, as He certainly taught, then how can we be content to go on year after year, doing virtually nothing to turn people to Him?

QUESTION 13

A Question of Preserving

"If the salt have lost his savour, wherewith shall it be salted?" (Matthew 5:13).

Christ, in His famous *Sermon on the Mount* (Matthew 5-7)—first so called by St. Augustine—asked this burning question. He replied to His own question by saying, "It is thenceforth good for nothing, but to be cast out, and to be trodden under foot of men."

These are burning words: *good for nothing . . . cast out . . . trodden under foot. . . .* This was meant to apply not to salt, which had merely served as the figure of speech, but to *men* who could have come to some much higher mark and nobler ending in life than this.

Salt, as here used, is a figure of *preservation.* This is one of the greatest needs for salt. It is reported to be scientifically certain that should all the salt suddenly disappear from the earth, the oceans of the warmer climes would soon stagnate. This would spread to the entire waters of earth, and the whole earth would in time become a mass of degenerating putrefaction, creating an atmosphere in which no form of life would be possible. So far as is known, there is *no substitute for salt* in the world.

Christ meant to make this plain to His followers—that as salt is the major preservative of life on earth, so His followers were to become the saving preservative of mankind. They were to become the "salt of the earth."

Salt is mentioned 33 times in the Bible. It is said that all forms of salt are good for about 14,000 uses. It is typical of good influence or the power of good in a society. Jesus referred to His followers as the "salt of the earth." Beyond doubt, the influence of Christianity has made possible the extension of our civilization this far into time. When Christ came into the world, civilization was decaying. Mankind was degenerating to the lowest levels. Morally, man was sinking into a caldron of an almost hopeless dilemma. The greatest civilizations of the past had sunken; the Roman Empire was headed into oblivion, and the lower forms of paganism were reigning supremely. The heathen religions had sunken into practices of the most unmentionable immorality. Temple prostitutes attached to most oriental religions had made their followers little more than the lowest of sensualists. Literature was corrupted and art was stained with this same vein of immorality.

The Christian religion with its message of purity and spiritual life brought the world a glorious new way of life. It gave mankind a powerful new lease upon life and brought to civilization its greatest hope. Christianity today is the last good hope for mankind! There is power in the pure, unadulterated message of Christ. We should get it to the nations of earth as fast as possible!

The Saviour painted a sad picture of salt which had "lost its savour." In Palestine there was a "Valley of Salt" which has been described as comparing to this metaphor. The protruding parts of the rock-like salt still retained its sparkle and whiteness, but the elements had drained away its saltiness. When one tasted this exposed part, he tasted only a flat, saltless gritty substance. Only back to where the salt adhered to the original salt rock was there saltiness. Just so, men exposed to the elements of the world, and losing contact with Christ the Rock, lose their spiritual life. They may still glitter with witty expression, and sparkle with worldly wisdom, but the spiritual unction and gracious inward power, that gives *life* to their profession, are gone.

Possibly the salt "trodden under foot" to which Christ referred was from the lake, Asphaltities, in Judea, which was bituminous salt. It was tasteless, and had no use, except to keep men from slipping on the pavements.

Let these words sink deeply into your heart—*good for nothing . . . cast out . . . trodden under foot*! Remember, such is the Lord's description of those professing Christians which have lost the saltiness of a genuine attachment to Him.

QUESTION 14

A Question of a Name

"What is thy name?" Mark 5:9.
One of the most pathetic stories of the Gospels is that of the poor demoniac of Gadara. Jesus had been teaching on the other side of the Sea of Galilee. Later that day they started for Gadara, when they encountered the fearful storm and Christ calmed the waves.

Upon reaching the coast of Gadara, they were met by a wild man out of the tombs, possessed of demons. He had been separated from society and left to roam in the wilderness-like countryside.

Reference to the "tombs" establishes somewhat the identity of the place. Jews buried their dead, usually outside the cities, lest they be contaminated by contacting a grave. Often they carved out tombs in the sides of the hills, and the bodies were placed in these to decompose. These tombs were sometimes large enough to accommodate extra persons who may care to shelter there.

The place of this scene was probably on the side of a rather steep mountain which came right down to the seashore. Likely the demon-possessed man dwelling in the high hillside had witnessed the dreadful storm and its sudden calming. As the boat landed he went to meet the sailors, probably being drawn to them by this strange incident. This display of divine power may have impelled some inner desire within him to contact whoever had been responsible for it. Upon seeing Jesus it appears the denons within him assumed the prerogative and cried for mercy.

Mark's account presents but one demoniac, while Matthew and Luke mention two. Mark likely selected the more fierce and dangerous of the two for special mention. It is doubtless the same account in all three Gospels, differing in minor details only.

Christ asked the man, "What is thy name?" Instantly he replied, "My name is Legion; for we are many." "Legion" was a term referring to a group of Roman soldiers, numbering about six thousand. It was used here to indicate the large number of demons and possibly their fierceness.

The rendering of the word "devils" here in the King James and other versions, as well as many other places in the New Testament, is unfortunate. There is but one Devil, Satan, "the Prince of the power of the air," the Adversary. This word should always be rendered *demon* or *demons,* as it is fron an entirely different Greek word than is the word correctly rendered "devil." The former is from *demonia* and its various forms, the latter from *Diabolous.*

There are many demons, untold in number anywhere in Scripture. It is generally believed that these consist of the fallen angels which fell with Lucifer, who became Satan, the Devil. Some of the worst of these appear to have been bound permanently by God (II Pet. 2:4; Jude 6), while others were allowed to remain free to work with Satan in his program of revenge against God and the destruction of man.

This man was not merely insane—he was much more. He was actually possessed of demons until he had lost the power of self-control entirely. In true demon possession, often diseases are present which aggravate the situation, as a result of the possession. Cases of demon possession are still reported sometimes in mission lands where the power of Satan is more fully asserted.

Christ asked for a confession of this man's name, that he might thereby *confess* the *nature* of his *needs.* Confession of need is always associated with any form of deliverance from sin or its results. This is strongly indicated by St. John: "If we *confess our sins*, he is faithful and just to forgive us our sins, and to cleanse us from all unrighteousness" (I John 1:9). Here forgiveness and cleansing are conditioned upon acknowledgment by *confession.* Confession of *need* is part of Christ's requirements for victory over sin.

QUESTION 15

A Question of Reading

"What is written in the law? How readest thou?" Luke 10:26.

Jesus had conmended His disciples for the fact that their names were written in heaven. He wished them to see that a proper relationship to God meant far more than to have great power for doing good.

Following this address to the disciples, a lawyer in the crowd wanted to know just what he could do to "inherit eternal life."

Jesus was never "caught off guard." He recognized instantly the hypocrisy and sham of the man, who was probably one of the Jerusalem leaders working to "trap" Him in His teachings.

The term "lawyer" referred generally to those scribes who *interpreted the meaning* of the law of Israel to the people. This is possibly why Christ shot back at him so forcefully the double question heading this chapter.

These pointed, personal questions were probably not expected by the smart lawyer. Perhaps he anticipated a "discourse" of some kind in which he could find some unorthodox statement to carry back to his superiors against Jesus. Christ may also have pointed to the small box-like container which the scribes wore on the wrist and sometimes on the forehead, containing a tiny scroll of the law of Moses, when He asked these questions.

The Master's disarming questions further placed the *lawyer* on the spot. Jesus asked, "What does the law say about this question you have just asked? How do you *interpret* it?" Christ switched the responsibility. "You are a professional interpreter of the law, what is the answer?"

Stunned for a moment at the suddenness with which Christ pummeled him—while the audience possibly laughed at him—the lawyer thought quickly. Replying, he quoted the *Deuteronomy* version of the first commandment, adding that one must also love his neighbor as himself. Jesus responded that he had answered right, and if he would do this he would have eternal life.

The lawyer pressed the question further, asking, "Who is my neighbor?" The Saviour responded with one of the most beautiful and compassionate stories in any literature in the world—the famous "Good Samaritan" story. This answered all quibblers for all time about who one's neighbor really is. It set the lawyer back on his heels, sending him home without further questions.

On the question of reading, it is amazing what some people "read into" the Word of God. The Jewish rabbis and their assistants, the scribes in particular, had added *traditions* to plain truths of the Word of God in the Old Testament. This applied largely to the Law of Moses, although certain other parts had not escaped. These "traditions" referred to by Christ, were really "interpretations" which the rabbis from ancient times had made of various Scriptures. Often in Old Testament versions these "explanations" were side by side with the original text. In this way they explained the meanings which had become attached to the Word. In some cases there were several varying explanations of the same text, often confusing the common reader as to the real meaning. In time these explanations became mixed in with the original inspired Word, so that it was difficult to separate them.

This is most likely what Jesus meant when He said once, "Thus have ye made the commandment of God of none effect by your tradition" (Matt. 15:6). (See Matt. 15:1-9 for an actual illustration of just what this system had done to the word of God.) There were about 600 of these *traditions,* or commentary explanations. Many times the people had accepted these instead of the Word of God on a given subject.

Is it not true even today that many "read into the Bible" the interpretation which suits them best? This can become tragic in one's life if allowed full sway.

QUESTION 16

A Question of Healing

"Wilt thou be made whole?" John 5:6.

There has been much discussion of this passage (John 5:1-9, particularly verse 4) by many learned commentators.

First, it is not known for certain to what "feast" John here refers, since he did not establish it by referring to a definite one. It has been referred to as the "second passover" feast by some; as that of "Purim," by others, and of "Dedication," or possibly the "Feast of Trumpets," by still others.

Some feel that Jesus' presence there and His address following the passage rule out the feasts of "Purim" and "Dedication," as they were wholly national in character and of no particular spiritual significance. Possibly the "Feast of Trumpets," commemorating Creation and the giving of the Law, is most likely referred to here.

Another problem is the pool of Bethesda. There are at least two different places cited by scholars which may have been this pool.

1. That of "Solomon's pool," or the "King's pool," referred to by Josephus. This was accepted by the great British Biblical lands research scholar, Robinson, as the one to which this is referring. It was near what is now St. Stephen's gate. This pool is known to have acted strangely, as if its waters were moving in a peculiar fashion. This was due to waters from the upper springs above it, casing into the pool by an underground tunnel which helped to feed the pool. It is also believed to have been affected by a reddish rock which colored its waters sometimes, and by certain iron chemicals which had healing properties in them. This may account for the references to the "moving" of the waters and also for reference to the sick and

tent folk lying nearby. There was also near this pool a columnar structure which may have answered to the "five porches" with covered roofing under which the sick are said to have waited.

2. Colonel Wilson, an early explorer in Palestine, however, was of the opinion that the pool was located by what was known as the ancient "Sheepgate," near which there was a spring, now covered by St. Anne's Church. He thinks *Siloam* and *Bethesda* may have been the same; and that the four old pillars in the east wall, together with the four pillars in the center, may answer the description of the "porches."

The site of the real pool is of little importance. The real knotty problem is the reference to the "angel troubling the waters" (John 5:4). Numbers of conservative, orthodox New Testament scholars have held that this verse is most likely an *interpolation*. It is perfectly possible that this was merely an ancient Jewish tradition—that an angel troubled the waters at a certain time—for there are many similar traditions. Ancient commentators may have inserted it into the text, as part of it, since it was so closely associated. It was then allowed to remain by early translators as part of the original text. In this way this passage may have come to be accepted as part of the original text when it should have been left as only a commentator's note.

By reading verses 3 and 5, skipping 4 altogether, one will see the perfect continuity of the passage, and that verse 4 actually sounds like an added comment. It could well be placed in parenthesis, and was likely so intended originally.

At the end of verse 5, Christ asked tne impotent man, "Wilt thou be made whole?" Here is a serious question of healing. For 38 years this poor man had probably lived near this pool, believing as many evidently did, that its waters had healing virtues. But always upon his arrival either the waters were not troubled, or he could get no one to place him into the pool; hence, he was denied its benefits. No miracle had occurred to him. Perhaps his faith was beginning to weaken when Jesus asked him the above question. In response, he looked up, believing in Jesus to help him, and a moment later, raised his voice in a triumphant victory shout.

Jesus Christ is still asking the multitudes today, "Wilt thou be made whole?" It is a mistake for God's people to neglect the privilege of bodily healing as offered in the New Testament, just because a few have gone to excess in this matter. Those who will exercise faith may still have the blessings promised in this passage, if they will but apply for it in the manner prescribed by James (James 5:13-15).

QUESTION 17

A Question of Discernment

"But whom say ye that I am?" Mark 8:29.

Jesus was near the city of Caesarea Philippi when He asked this question.

This city was located near Mount Libanus and was called *Dan* in ancient times (Gen. 14:14). Its new name, Caesarea Philippi, was given to it by Philip, the tetrarch, who ruled that region some time before the days of Christ and had built the city. He named it Caesarea, in honor of Tiberius Caesar, then the Roman Emperor. The name Philippi was attached to distinguish it from another Caesarea on the Mediterranean Sea, and doubtless, also, that the name of the ruling tetrarch may be preserved as its builder.

A national stir had occurred among the Jewish leaders and common people about Jesus and His work. Some believed He was the greatest of all the prophets, others hoped He was the Messiah. Some considered Him a harmless, other-worldly rabbi dreamer whose teachings were unrealistic. Only a few considered Him a dangerous political figure, contending for a position of rulership. But a powerful core of the temple priests and leaders set out to destroy Him and would not stop until it was finished.

One reason for the opposition of the religious leaders was Jesus' constant ministry, the plain truth of which always left them smarting under its disagreeable penetrations of their falsity and shame. He minced no words. He publically exposed their sins, laid bare their utter hypocrisies and showed the flimsy spinelessness of their lives.

Back and forth across Palestine Christ moved, preaching, healing, casting out demons and exposing the sinfulness of the nation. He often pointed to its evils with caustic words, painfully revealing statements and burning, unanswered questions. His manner, words of truth and gracious manifestations of divine compassion and power convinced people everywhere that He was not an ordinary man.

As His ministry spread, the conviction of His divine mission grew. Some even thought of Him as the Son of God. This was quite dangerous talk for if He were not the Son of God, then it was horrible blasphemy. If He was, then they were making a fearful mistake in not recognizing Him!

Knowing the disciples had unanswered questions, Jesus asked them frankly at Caesarea Philippi, "But whom say ye that I am?" Some gave differing answers.

But Peter, as spokesman, replied in the words of immortal fame, "Thou art the Christ, the Son of the living God" (Matt. 16:16). Christ assured Peter that the truth he had spoken was inspired by the heavenly Father, who had made this revelation to Peter.

Following this "Great Confession," Christ assured the disciples that the Christian Church was to be built upon this very foundation. Jesus did not tell Peter that His Church would be founded upon *him*. He did not even indicate that Peter should in any sense become its chief ruler. It was upon the truth of Christ's eternal Sonship as the Son of God, and its redemptive mission and purpose, that the Church was to be built upon (Matt. 16:18).

Christ's eternal Sonship as God's Son is so basic to Christianity that without it Christianity would crumble to the dust. This great cardinal doctrine is the Keystone in the arch of God's truth, and of the whole structure of Christianity. It is the source of all the redemptive work of Christ, and the cornerstone of every believer's saving faith.

QUESTION 18

A Question of Fragments

"How many baskets full of fragments took ye up?" Mark 8:19.

Jesus had recently performed the miracle of feeding the multitude in Galilee from a few loaves and fishes. He and the disciples had now sailed over the Sea of Galilee to the part of the country known as Magdala. This place is referred to as "Dalmanutha" by Mark, in the similar account. It may be possible that either this latter name was formed by changing arrangement of letters in Magdala and adding the Syric termination, *atha;* or more likely, that Magdala was the *country* while Dalmanutha was the coastal *city* of the little strip of country.

Upon arriving, Jesus warned His disciples about the dangers of the pernicious doctrines of the scribes and Pharisees. He said, "Beware of the leaven of the Pharisees, and of the leaven of Herod" (Mark 8:15). He chose the symbol of "leaven," working in meal or bread dough to make it rise, until the whole loaf was fully filled with the leaven. This, He said, was like the wickedness of these corrupt leaders. Working quietly but powerfully, their corrupting influence would continue until the whole nation was poisoned by it. He may have had in mind not only the general principle, but His own particular case. These leaders would work slowly, silently, deceitfully, until they had turned the whole nation against Him and the gospel He preached. This would culminate in His death.

To paraphrase His words, "Watch, that *you* are not overcome and lead away with this subtle, cunning planning. Be careful that you are not caught in this same trap, and in the end find yourselves forsaking and turning against Me, and siding with the enemies of God and truth." This was a stern, but needful warning.

The disciples still did not get His point. The wicked leaders had so well concealed their plans that even His best friends were not always aware of the traps being set for Him and themselves.

In this light, the disciples thought He was upbraiding them for not bringing sufficient bread for this particular trip. They were secretly discussing their failure to have acted prudently in this matter. Recognizing their mistake, He corrected them by putting the question about feeding the multitudes to them, "How many baskets full of fragments took ye up?"

Turning to the question of "fragments," note: 1. The *economy* of Jesus. "That nothing be wasted." This He applies to human life and physical situations. These fragments were useful leftovers; they would provide the people with future sustenance on their ways homeward.

Because the universe abounds with plenteousness is no reason for wastefulness. This should be applied to our daily lives. Nothing should be utterly wasted and destroyed if usable.

2. Christ teaches us the economy of *time,* and the savableness of precious energies which used properly can add much to His kingdom and our good. The average person can secure a complete university education in the spare time that is generally "wasted."

Some of the great works of literature, art, inventions, and valuable contributions to science, industry and human progress have been made by people working in their *spare time*. We should save up the "fragments" of life, and use them to the best possible advantages. Let no one say that he cannot do this or that, for lack of *time,* until he has utilized all the *fragments* which others cast away.

3. Our Lord may have wished to demonstrate through these "fragments" that this miracle was *genuine*. It was no momentary trick of magic, or psychological method of making

the people feel they were satisfied because of the utter unselfishness of those "sharing" their small bit with the multitude. The bread and fish actually multiplied in our Lord's hands as He broke and passed it along. There was plenty left over, to convince anyone who cared to look. It was also of such a tangible nature that it could stand up to careful scrutiny and scientific examination.

This lesson remains for us today, "Save the *fragments*" of all of life and time. Make the most of them, for out of them may come the greatest good of life.

QUESTION 19

A Question of Faith

"Where is your faith?" Luke 8:25. "When the Son of man cometh, shall he find faith on the earth?" Luke 18:8.

These two questions of the Master about faith grew out of the fears of the disciples in the midst of the Galilean storm; and as a result of His story about the poor widow and the unjust judge.

Christ had finished teaching on the shore of the lake of Galilee and requested the disciples to go to the other side of the lake, possibly for a rest. The "Sea of Galilee" is a pear-shaped basin about thirteen miles long and eight miles wide. It is situated right down between the mountains of Israel on one side and the hills of Moab on the other. The Jordan River empties into it at the upper end and runs out of it at the lower end, thus feeding the lake and making it possible. Quick-rising winds from the nearby hills often moved down upon this lake, churning its waters into sudden squalls and heaping them up in dreadful billows. It was such a storm as this which they had encountered that day.

Jesus, asleep in the cabin of the little boat at the back end, was undisturbed. Finally, in desperation, the disciples awoke Him. He arose and quieted the storm. Turning to the disciples, He said simply, *"Where is your faith?"*

They marveled at His wondrous power, but may they not have wondered even more at His piercing question, "Where is *your* faith?" Perhaps they said, "Why, He talked as if He actually expected *us* to calm that storm!" Or maybe they felt He asked them, rather, "What are you worried about? Where is your faith? You don't think I will allow the ship to go down

— 47 —

while I am on board with you, do you?" He could possibly have meant both of these.

It seems a bit difficult to believe that He expected His yet immature followers to actually command storms to be calmed and get results. And yet, He was to send them out to cast out demons, and even to "raise the dead." What more then could be expected of them? It is entirely possible that had they ventured to rebuke the storm in His name, it would have subsided.

The second question the Master asked concerned faith for importunate prayer (Luke 18:8). Christ pictured a poor widow calling ceaselessly upon a hard-hearted old judge until he avenged her of her enemy. He said this was like the loving Heavenly Father, who would avenge His elect though He bore long with them. Now, He turns to the application. To paraphrase His question, "When the Son of man comes back to earth to claim His saints, will He find *this kind of faith*—the faith of *importunate, ceaseless, intercessory prayer?*"

Some Bible scholars have thought the answer to this question is no. It seems that some element of this kind of faith is necessary, however, for the believer to remain in a state of grace and spiritual life. Certainly, Christ will find saints upon the earth when He comes. But will this kind of extraordinary *prevailing* prayer be found at large?

The Church today is in sore need of this type of faith and of the prevailing, intercessory prayer that accompanies it.

QUESTION 20

A Question of Murder

"Why go ye about to kill me?" John 7:19.

Jesus had only shortly before healed the man who had been afflicted for 38 years. People were marveling at this miracle and His mighty power over disease. But the Jewish leaders were out to discredit and destroy Him.

By healing the man on the Sabbath and telling him to take his bed and walk to his house, Jesus had supposedly violated the law of the Sabbath. A man in Moses' time for only gathering wood for moking a fire had received the death penalty for this offense. The Jewish leaders, therefore, wished to use this as a lawful reason for destroying Jesus. But Jesus promptly took cover under "the law of mercy," as He did once before by explaining that if an ox should be stuck in a ditch on the Sabbath, they would pull him out. Since this was an act of mercy, and therefore acceptable, was not healing this man much more an act of mercy, and acceptable to be done on the Sabbath? He also inquired, did they not circumcise a child on the Sabbath? This rite required far more work than the mere pronouncing of a healing blessing upon a sick man, or the man walking a short way to his home, carrying his little mattress pad. They could not counteract much reasoning.

To turn the tide before the people had a chance to reason this all out, the Jewish leaders shouted at Him, "You are mad; you are possessed of a demon!" If He were insane as is the meaning here; or if possessed of a demon, then He could not be trusted as a teacher of the people. They intended to kill His influence and break His power with the people.

The King James version here says the "people" said He was mad and had a demon, but several old manuscript versions have it rather, "The Jews said. . . ." This doubtless lays the matter correctly upon the Jewish leaders who sought to destroy Him. It was under these circumstances that Jesus asked the Jewish leaders, "Why go ye about to kill me?" In other words, "Why are you trying to kill Me for simply doing the same kind of good works on the Sabbath as you yourselves do? If I am of God, why do you persecute Me? Why do you not hear God's Word as I have spoken it to you?"

At another time He informed the people that they desired His destruction because the love of God was not in them. They knew only the narrow confines of a legalistic religion. They were blind to the deep spiritual truths of God. They wished to be let alone in their smug complacency and sins. Jesus' burning words cut their hearts to the quick, making them uncomfortable and often showing them up before the people as hypocrites and false pretenders. They could stand their own heart's condemnation, but when He discredited them *before the public*, this meant the end of the road, for they determined to kill Him.

Question 21

A Question of Accusers

"Woman, where are those thine accusers? hath no man condemned thee" John 8:10.

The Jewish leaders were eager to trap Christ in embarrassing situations that they might be able to bring Him into public reproach. They brought a woman whom they claimed to have found in the act of adultery. Quoting Moses, who ordered death in such cases, they asked Jesus for His opinion.

As if He did not hear them, He stooped and wrote upon the ground—the only instance we have of His writing anything. When they kept clamoring for a reply, He rose, looked them squarely in the eyes, and said, "He that is without sin among you, let him first cast a stone." Then He stooped and wrote again upon the ground. The accusers all went out one by one.

Looking at the poor embarrassed woman, Jesus asked, "Woman, where are those thine accusers? hath no man condemned thee?" She replied, "No man, Lord." Then He admonished her, "Neither do I condemn thee: go, and sin no more."

The following facts are important: Moses set the rule for stoning those guilty of adultery. This was severe, but it preserved the morality of the nation. One of the ways adulterers in ancient times were punished was by placing the culprit on a scaffold ten or twelve feet high, half naked, with hands tied behind the back. She would then be pushed off suddenly. If the fall served to kill her completely, nothing further was done. If not, one of the "witnesses" which were required to be present, took a huge stone and hurled it down upon her breast, which was generally the finishing stroke. This method was not always followed, however, as the reference to stoning the woman above indicates.

Jesus said, "Let him that is without sin among you first cast a stone." The Greek from which the words "without sin" are taken, means *the same kind of sin*. "He who has not been guilty of adultery, let him start stoning her." is a good paraphrase. Not a man in the group could respond. How often those who are guilty of the *same sins as others*, cry loudest for their condemnation.

Christ's words, "Neither do I condemn thee," must be understood within their context. He did not *condone* the woman! His meaning, against the background of their request for her stoning, is, "Neither do I condemn thee *to death*, as these men would have done. Go now, and mend you way, and do not indulge in this sin any more."

Here we have an example of the loving mercy of our Lord. He is willing to help the weak and sinful to find peace and restoration to God's favor, as He demonstrated on other occasions: "For the Son of man is come to seek and to save that which was lost" (Luke 19:10). "The Son of man came not to destroy men's lives, but to save them."

QUESTION 22

A Question of Kindred

"Who is my mother? and who are my brethren?" Matthew 12:48.

Jesus had pronounced some of His sternest truths to His disciples and the questioning, agitating Pharisees. In the midst of His discourse, someone in the audience interrupted, informing Him that His mother and brethren had just arrived. He asked His informant, "Who is my mother? and who are my brethren?" Pointing toward His apostles and disciples, He replied to His own question: "Whoosoever shall do the will of my Father which is in heaven, the same is my brother, and sister, and mother" (Matt. 12:50).

Some believe "brethren" here referred to only "cousins," as it was common among the Hebrews of this time to speak of cousins as *brethren*. Mark 3:31 refers to them as His relatives. If this is true then they were most likely the sons of either Mary's sister, the wife of Alpheus, or of Mary, the wife of Cleopas. Others believe that Mary had other children besides Jesus and these were literally His brothers, sons of Mary and Joseph. This would certainly seem consistent with the passage where the angel told Joseph to fear not to take Mary to wife; that her child was conceived of the Holy Ghost. Then follows the statement that he "knew her not till she had brought forth her first born son." This plainly indicates that he lived with her as a normal wife thereafter. The reference to Christ as the "first born son" may also indicate that there were other younger sons; otherwise, what is the meaning of "first born son"?

The notion that Mary had no other children and that Joseph lived with her as a sister, she being too holy to partake of the lowly experiences of marital life, is utterly without foundation. This doctrine paves the way for the *assumption of Mary*, raising her to the status of a divine being to be worshipped. This is both pagan and idolatrous and must be rejected as utterly unscriptural. This instance shows the dangers of the doctrine that the Church, not the Bible, has the last word in divine revelation. Since the Church produced the New Testament, it is argued, therefore, the Church has the authority through its Councils, to add to the sum of divine revelation whatever it may choose. Revelation, then, is not completed, but continuous through the Church.

This is the theological basis for such changes and additions in doctrines as the Church of Rome has made from time to time. One can see immediately to what this heresy may lead, as in this case of *Mariolitry,* or the worship of Mary.

The ancient pagan religions, in their lowest forms, had *female deities* associated with their worship. This further debased the worship by introducing among the adherents immoral sex practices. Pagan Christianity seems to be following this trend.

Who are Christ's brothers, sisters, and even mothers, in the meaning of His language that day? This language was figurative, but the truth is just as forceful as if it had been literal. Christ answered His own question as He often did. Whosoever does the will of God, follows Jesus as Saviour and Lord, knows the kinship of God through faith in Christ and by His redeeming power and grace—these are His brethren and sisters, and mothers.

QUESTION 23

A Question of Who Is My Neighbor

"Which now . . . thinkest thou, was neighbour unto him that fell among the thieves?" Luke 10:36.

When Jesus was teaching one day a certain scribe asked, "Who is my neighbour?" Jesus told him that God required man to love God with all his heart and his neighbor as himself. According to the Jews, they were neighbors only to the Jews. One could allow a Gentile to die nearby without ministering to him, and still be blameless before the Jews.

Christ turned the tables in His famous story of the Good Samaritan. The Samaritans were hated by the Jews, as outcasts from Israel. Now Jesus used the Good Samaritan story to bring home the truth that anyone near you who is in distress and need, is indeed your neighbor, irrespective of race, creed or circumstances!

The following things are of interest in answering the neighbor question:

1. The Greek word translated "neighbour" actually means "one who is near"; in its literal sense it meant not only *near*, but also one who *dwells* near, or *passes near*. In the old Anglo-Saxon, which preceded modern English, the word meant next. One next to you. This means that anyone who lives near you, or is passing near you, or whom you may pass, who is in need of your services, mercy or kindness, has the claim upon it; just as you would upon him in a similar circumstance.

2. Our neighbors, then, in Christ's meaning are not merely our friends or our pals. Rather, anyone who may chance to come or be near to us, who for any reason needs our care, sympathy and help is our neighbor.

3. The Jerusalem-Jericho road, mentioned here by our Lord, was the most highly traveled road in all Judea at this time. Judea was then infested with robber bands, which often fell upon travelers and robbed them. It is reported that some 12,000 priests and Levites lived in and around Jericho, and these were among the most constant travelers between Jericho and Jerusalem. It is most likely that this incident may have occured much as Jesus told it that day.

The Jews had the least right to expect anything from the Samaritans. Yet, Jesus tells of this Good Samaritan, who out of compassion and mercy, helped the wounded Jew, even after his own countrymen had bypassed him. He emphasized the fact that *love* needs no credentials of race or creed. Its only credentials are compassion and mercy, unselfishness and the desire to help another in time of need.

Some have supposed that this story may be spiritualized as follows: A certain man—*Adam*—went down—*from Jerusalem*, the height of spiritual life and perfection—*to Jericho*—meaning, his *"moon"*—a state of *transitory* and *changing existence*. Thieves—*sin and Satan*—stripped him—*of his righteousness*—and left him wounded—*affected in heart and life by sin*—half dead—possessing *a living body*, but a *dead soul*—"dead in trespasses and in sins."

The priest—*the moral law*—and the Levite—*the ceremonial laws*—passed by on the other side—*had no power to help him*. (Priests and Levites were ceremonially forbidden to touch dying people; so they could not help him, had they wanted to do so.) But a certain Samaritan—*Christ*—as He journeyed—*from heaven to the cross* to die for us—came near where He was—*put Himself in man's place*, became incarnate and bore man's sins—*had compassion on him*. Compassion is the heart of redemption's work. He *went* to *him*—*where he was*. (Christ came to seek and to save sinners, coming where we were.) He bound up his wounds—*in love and comforting promises*—pouring in oil—*in pardoning mercy*—and wine—*the fullness of the Holy Spirit's baptism and comforting power*—brought him to an inn—*the Church and the people of God*—who were to take care of him. He *gave two pence—law and gospel*—to the inn-keeper—*ministers* of the gospel—to convict of sin and offer mercy—*take care of him* as God's *minister* and *steward of grace*—I will repay thee—with everlasting rewards—when I come again—*at Christ's coming.*

If this analogy is used, it must be with *caution*. This is only a *possible* secondary application—a spiritualization. It is certainly not the main purpose of the story, as seen above. Christ meant to drive home the truth of who is one's neighbor, our responsibility to others in the light of His grace for all men, and our Christian heritage and the opportunity for helping others.

QUESTION 24

A Question of God's Giving

"If ye then, being evil, know how to give good gifts unto your children: how much more shall your heavenly Father give the Holy Spirit to them that ask him?" Luke 11:13.

Christ had been praying and His disciples, observing Him in prayer, now asked Him to teach them to pray. He presented to them a simple outline of general prayer (Luke 11:2-4). This is not a mere repetition of the *Matthew* outline of prayer (Matt. 6:5-15), but rather, a similar one. It is thought that the *Matthew* outline and explanation followed the second passover; this, possibly, came after the third, some year or so later. This may reveal how very slow the disciples had been to catch the significance of prayer and begin its practice.

This prayer outline is merely an *example* of the *nature* and *scope* of prayer. The arithmetic book is but examples to teach the student *how* to solve mathematical problems, and not the solution to all problems. So this prayer is merely the guidelines of *how* to *pray*.

Following this prayer outline, Jesus encouraged the disciples to trust the Father's love and willingness to answer their prayers. For this purpose He used several illustrations, such as the friend who answered because of the continual petitioning, and the father who would not give his child a scorpion for an egg, or a serpent for a fish. He climaxed His exhortation by asking one of the great questions of the New Testament which heads this chapter.

The compassion of God reaches out as far as the heavens are high above the earth. As much as the ocean is greater than the largest lake, or the Amazon River larger than its tributary springs, so there is no contrast great enough to measure it.

Jesus said God's tender compassion is like that of an earthly Father, only far superior.

Christian believers everywhere need to see the utmost importance of this blessed promise, relative to the Holy Spirit! The Church's greatest need is for all believers to be filled with the Holy Spirit; filled with a burning desire to win others to Christ, and a deep communion in prayer.

This calls for the emptying out of self in total commitment to Christ, that He may become the pre-eminent One in life. If the Church were so filled with the Holy Spirit, Christ's cause would immediately become first in every life, and the world would soon feel the powerful impact of such redeeming love and undying devotion.

QUESTION 25

A Question of Consequences

"Said I not unto thee, that, if thou wouldest believe, thou shouldest see the glory of God?" John 11:40.

The setting for this question is the death and entombment of Lazarus, at Bethany. Christ and His disciples were taking a much needed rest. He referred to Lazarus' sickness earlier, but He made no effort to go to Him. Two days later they started for Jerusalem which required a day or so's journey at best. On the way Jesus announced to His disciples that Lazarus was "dead."

The disciples could not understand why Jesus was going to Lazarus if he was already dead, nor the meaning of His words, "I go that I may wake him out of his sleep."

It seemed to Martha that He had arrived too late to do any good. But Christ moves upon a divine, not a human, schedule. We often feel with Mary, "Lord, if thou hadst been here . . ." such things would not have happened. How often we fail to see that Christ's ways and ours are not on the same level. He looks at things from the divine viewpoint from all that is best for us; whereas, we see only today, and often that very poorly. Who can know one hour, or even a few minutes beyond the present moment what is coming, or what will be best for us? Is it not therefore wise to commit ourselves and our future into the hands of a merciful and all-wise God?

When Mary and Martha voiced their disappointments and something of their faith for the future, Christ allowed the situation to sink in upon them. Christ was unperturbed at the scene of Lazarus' death. He knew the future—Martha and Mary did not!

Lazarus' grave was likely a cave in the hillside, with the doorway covered by a huge stone rolled against it. Jesus groaned in spirit when He came to it. Here is one of the most touching scenes of Jesus' earthly life, "Jesus wept." His great love for Lazarus and for Martha and Mary in their hour of grief was poured out in those tears of compassion.

At the graveside Martha halted when Christ asked that the stone of the door be removed. She complained that he had been dead now four days; it would therefore be both hopeless and embarrassing to open the tomb. But she heard Christ's words, "He that believeth in me, though he were dead, yet shall he live," but thought they applied only to future resurrection. Then Jesus asked the profound question, "Said I not unto thee, that, if thou wouldest believe, thou shouldest see the glory of God?"

Countless millions in trouble, and upon the verge of despair, need to hear this blessed message: *Christ knows the future and He knows what is best for all of us.*

What sorrow, heartache and lonely hours of anxiety could be saved for God's children, if they would only trust in this simple truth.

QUESTION 26

A Question of Commitment

"If therefore ye have not been faithful in the unrighteous mammon, who will commit to your trust the true riches?" Luke 16:11.

Christ told a story of how an unjust steward's master commended his prudence, though he condemned his actions, when the servant learned of his release from further service to his master. Christ observed that the people of the world are wiser than the "children of light"—or the Christians—in many instances. The Christian uses true wisdom of God in turning from sin to Christ, but is sometimes short-handed in the use of prudence and good judgment in his pursuance of Christian living. Worldlings are often more prudent in preparing for this life than the righteous are in carrying out their heavenly preparation.

Because of the poor rendering of this passage, Christ has been thought to be commending the unjust steward. Rather, He was condemning the righteous for their poor use of wisdom in eternal matters.

Making friends of the "unrighteous mammon" is also of special interest. "Mammon" means worldly riches. The *mammon of unrighteousness* would probably be better rendered, the "riches of injustice." Riches are often most "deceitful"; and in this sense, unjust. They begat hope only to bring despair; they promise pleasure, only to end in pain and disappointment.

The Saviour's words may probably be paraphrased in the following way: "Take the riches which you may gain in this life and use them to secure the eternal friendship of those whom you may win to God by their best use; then when you have finished your earthly life, these friends will welcome you into everlasting joy and pleasure, for having helped them to obtain eternal life" (Luke 16:9).

Christ then warns that if one cannot be trusted to use the riches of this life even in the smallest matters in ways of justice and righteousness, who could trust him with the riches of God which are far greater? If one is unfaithful in worldly affairs which are of least importance, how can he be trusted as a steward of heavenly things which are of eternal value?

The famous wealthy Rothchilds are reported to have had an alert, wide awake young man of more than average ability as one of their clerks in New Orleans. They had thought of preparing him for high responsibility in the company. At the time, he was in charge of buying and selling cotton. In a special test case, the Rothchild's directors ordered him to sell a certain amount of cotton on a certain day. Believing that he knew the local market better than his superiors, he waited four days and sold the cotton for a net profit of $40,000 *more* than he would have gotten had he sold when ordered. With jubilation he wired the sale to the home office. The next day he received a return wire saying: "The $40,000 is yours. Your successor sails tomorrow." In other words, he had disobeyed orders, and acted upon his own. Though he made them a lot of money, he proved by this action that he could not be trusted for higher responsibilities in the firm.

God wants to develop Christians who can be trusted to be *faithful* when they may not see nor understand *why*. "It is not mine to question the leadings of my Lord, it is but mine to follow the dictates of His Word."

QUESTION 27

A Question of Ownership

"But God said unto him, Thou fool, this night thy soul shall be required of thee: then whose shall those things be which thou hast provided?" Luke 12:20.

The story of the Rich Fool, as this passage has been called, contains a lot of helpful moral truth. Jesus told the story in response to the two brothers who had been quarreling over their estate and one had appealed to Him for advice in settling the matter (See Luke 12:14-17.)

After depicting the young farmer's progressive building programs, and the huge storages of wealth, the Master put His finger upon the sore spot of the whole thing. The young man had made provisions for his abounding crops, had looked into the future of his resourcefulness, and planned for all his life's entertainment for "many years" in advance. His whole life's creed was truly Epicurean—"eat, drink, be merry." He *made no plans* for spiritual development, and left God out of all his future plans.

God called a fearful halt to the haughty man's plans: "But God said unto him, Thou fool, this night thy soul shall be required of thee: then whose shall those things be which thou hast provided?"

This story illustrates the proper nature of ownership and is a supreme lesson in stewardship. Few people have a proper concept of their relationship to this life. The average person feels that whatever he has is his, and no one has any right to say anything about it. Few recognize that man has nothing which he can properly call his own—not even his soul. God has declared in His Word, "All souls are mine" (Ezekiel 18:4). Even the very breath in our nostrils is God's gift, and can be taken away any instant He may see fit. In the last analysis, we possess absolutely *nothing* of our *own*.

Man literally possesses nothing; yet, he is fully responsible for his actions while passing through this life. St. Paul affirmed, "For we brought nothing into this world, and it is certain we can carry nothing out" (I Tim. 6:7). One can take with him from this earth only whatever moral and spiritual values he has gained here. Job realized this when he cried, "Naked came I . . . naked shall I return . . . the Lord gave, and the Lord hath taken away . . ." (Job 1:21).

Man is only a steward on God's earth, and must one day give an account of his stewardship. Atheist, agnostic, unbeliever, or obedient believer, will make no difference. We must all appear before God's judgment seat to give an account and receive our just reward or punishment.

The Rich Fool makes ten references to himself in his plans, and not one reference to God. Here is utter selfishness at its height. Sam P. Jones, great southern Methodist evangelist of a former generation, once said, "A man who will sit down to his table before his children and eat, without returning thanks to the good Provider of all things . . . all the human in him has turned to hog, and he is at best eleven tenths hog!"

A young man was sent to college by a good benefactor. In his senior year, he returned to thank the older man for his kindness. "What are your plans, young man?" asked his older friend.

"Well, I plan to finish college, attend law school, then hang out my shingle and practice law, like you, Sir," said the young man.

"Fine, and what then?" the older man asked.

"Well, I hope to marry, have a family and educate them as you have me," he said.

"Fine, what next?" asked the older man.

"Well, I hope to make a good fortune and retire comfortably," said the younger.

"Fine, fine; what then?" the older man probed still further.

"Well, I guess then I shall be an old man and finally die," admitted the younger man.

The old man's eyes flashed fire as they penetrated the soul of the younger man; he cried, as he pounded his office desk, "My God, young man, and *what then?*"

This youngster had planned the exact course of the Rich Fool—no plans for Christ, no room for God in his whole career.

Take one last glance at this poor deluded soul when he came so suddenly into judgment. From all evidences he was still a young man when called to meet his Maker. Note the judgment of God upon him: It was a *personal* judgment—"thou fool"; it was an *immediate* judgment—"this night"; it was a *costly* judgment—"thy soul."

How truly has someone remarked, "The weakest spot in every man is where he thinks himself the wisest."

QUESTION 28
A Question of Ability

"Ye know not what ye ask: can ye drink of the cup that I drink of? and be baptized with the baptism that I am baptized with?" Mark 10:38.

Much comment has been made about the mother of James and John coming to Jesus to make a special request for them. The boys may have persuaded her to do this on their behalf. Anyhow, she came to ask that when Christ came into His kingdom, James and John be granted the privilege to sit on the right and left hand of Christ, helping Him to administer kingdom affairs.

Whether out of confidence in her sons' abilities, or of motherly love submitting to their pleas, one must admit this was certainly a great venture on her part. Had she achieved the purpose, it would have been a tremendous accomplishment for her and her sons!

We should be cautious before condemning her action. True mothers always wish the best for their children, and often have extravagant confidence in their abilities.

There can be little question but that her sons had the worldly ambition to become leaders in the kingdom of Christ. Such prominence would give them positions of power and prestige. How often have men mistaken religious ambition for Christian piety! To get ahead in the Church or state has many times been a hindrance rather than a help to good men. The other disciples were little better at heart than James and John, as seen in their being "much displeased" at these brethren.

The Saviour recognized that it was the sons in reality who were making the request, and asked them the question of this chapter. They replied in the affirmative. Jesus explained that they would indeed be baptized with His baptism and drink of His cup, but their *request* could only be granted by God who had reserved it for those most worthy.

Christians often fail to realize fully what they ask for in prayer. These brethren had not the faintest idea of the cup of Gethsemane and Calvary, nor yet of the baptism of Pentecost. The latter was a glorious fulfullment of promise, but it could come only after the former. Without Gethsemane and Calvary, there could have been no Pentecost with power and rejoicing.

Without the crises of the Christian life—its sufferings, prayers, self-denials, and full surrenders to Christ and His dsands upon one—there can be no Christian triumph, no power in service nor testimony of personal victory in Christ. No cup and cross means no crown nor palm of victory!

QUESTION 29

A Question of Going

"Whither goest thou?" John 16:5.

The occasion of this question was the after supper address of our Lord to His disciples as recorded by St. John. It seems likely that Jesus spoke the whole discourse listed in John 13-16, and the prayer in 17, at this time in connection with the passover feast. Note the following facts in support of this idea:

1. Chapter 13 opens with the passover supper, the washing of feet and the general remarks of Christ about His betrayal and death. The story of the institution of the Lord's supper is passed over entirely. Supposedly this is because John knew Matthew, Mark and Luke had all set forth this story. He, therefore, omits this to record other important details of Christ's teachings. Beginning with chapter 13 he goes consecutively without a break to the close of the prayer in chapter 17.

2. Chapter 18 opens with the remark that "when he had spoken these words, he went forth with his disciples" into the garden of Gethsemane. In this remark we are assured that all of chapters 13 through 17 is one long discourse, punctuated by personal references, and by the really *true* "Lord's Prayer" (chapter 17), for the sanctification of His apostles and followers for all time to come. This great High Priestly Prayer was evidently prayed, *not in the garden*, but in this large upper room where the passover feast was held.

3. It seems likely that this whole transaction, the lecture to faithfulness, warnings against forsaking Him, comforting words of John 14-16, and the final "Dedicatory Prayer," took place somewhere between sunset and midnight on Thursday evening of the dawn of the Passover. A closer look at this whole passage—13-17—discloses a unity of thought and purpose

throughout. These may truly be said to be the *parting words* of our Lord, looking back from the portals of death.

In the midst of this evening of "togetherness," with its deep pall of gloom for His departing words, and bright skies of promise for His future return, there occurs the short question of this chapter. After telling them all the things about His coming death and resurrection, He says, "But now I go my way to him that sent me: and none of you asketh me, Whither goest thou?" Both Peter and Thomas had asked almost this identical question earlier (13:36; 14:6), but *now* they were asking no further questions.

Why had they not asked any more questions? Had Christ previously answered their questions sufficiently? Or, despairing and hopeless, did they feel that no question asked would receive the much desired answer they hoped for?

Why did the Saviour ask this question? Perhaps His human nature called it forth in that hour of sorrow and grief. Possibly He longed for their fellowship and understanding. He wanted their devotion and trust. Questions asked by those of lesser importance in a friendship are often but evidence of their love and trust. Christ welcomes our questions about our needs and His work, even today.

QUESTION 30

A Question of Knowing

"Know ye what I have done?" John 13:12.

John 13 opens as if the passover supper was the first event on the calendar, as listed in the King James version. However, it is thought that the words in verse two, "Supper being ended," may better be rendered from the Greek, "while supper was being prepared."

According to ancient Jewish practice, the feet were washed before the meal. They washed the feet sometimes upon entering the home. When there was to be a meal, the feet of the guests were washed before the meal, as they were likely to be soiled from the dusty streets, since only open sandals of some type were worn then. The feet were often placed upon a divan, the persons lying in a half sitting or reclining position. DeVinci's Lord's Supper, with Christ and His apostles all "seated" in medieval or modern style, around the table, is far from what the original scene was actually like.

The foot-washing scene at the beginning of the passover meal, served by our Lord and His disciples, was likely not at midnight, but early in the evening. Those who prefer to follow the King James translation, and think of the scene as coming at the *end* of the passover meal, and *before* the institution of the Lord's Supper, find this time most acceptable for the foot-washing. It precedes the institution of the gracious "Lord's Supper," which has been a highlight in Christian worship, throughout the Christian centuries.

Christ disrobed Himself of His outward mantle, and girded Himself with a towel for the purpose of the foot-washing. This was the same type of towel used by the slaves for this purpose. In the wealthier homes, only slaves did this most menial task of washing the guests' feet. This practice, too, was reserved for the very lowest of the slaves. It was thought of as the lowest form of service one could render to another. Without a word of explanation, Christ took the basin, tied the towel about Him, and started washing the disciples' feet. The awestricken disciples must have been dumbfounded, wondering what He meant to do or teach them. From such menial service to him from his Lord, Peter drew back in horror. When Jesus reminded him that unless he submitted to this, he had no part with Him, he cried, "Not my feet only, but my hands and my head also."

When Jesus finished, He looked at the disciples, and asked, *"Know ye what I have done?"* He then said, to paraphrase it, "You call me Lord and Master, and this is correct; if I have washed your feet, you should also be big enough to wash each others' feet. Stop quibbling about who is the most important and will hold the largest office or place in the Kingdom. Let this lesson of humility soak into your souls. I have set you an example of the attitude you are to show to your brethren and others whom you are to serve in the work of the kingdom. You are to be 'servants,' not overlords, in My kingdom. Only as you are willing to be servants to all men can you win them to Me, and go out and build up My kingdom."

This is the substance of all He did and said. He did not establish an "ordinance" to wash each other's feet, ceremonially; though none should object if some wish to do this. This may become a dead ceremony, and one may wash the feet of a brother for whom he would not perform some *other* equally menial task the next day, with good grace!

Here is a profound lesson in morals and ethics, rather than in ceremony. This is the heart of the Christian Gospel. Jesus said, "By this shall all men know that ye are my disciples if ye have love one to another." *Not* if you wash each other's feet, are baptized by this or that mode, or receive the sacraments, but rather, *"if ye have love one to another."* This is the badge of true discipleship.

QUESTION 31

A Question of Willingness

"Wilt thou lay down thy life for my sake?" John 13:38.

This question is found among the scenes of the last hours of Christ on earth. He told the disciples in the upper room "discourse" what would soon befall Him. Peter asked why he could not follow Him into that mysterious bourne, for Peter did not then understand what Christ meant. Told again that he could not follow Him, Peter ventured, "I will lay down my life for thy sake."

Looking earnestly at Peter, Jesus asked, "Wilt thou lay down thy life for my sake?" "That is good and noble, Peter," to paraphrase Christ's words, "but I tell you truly that before the cock crows for daybreak, you will have denied Me three times."

What stunning words these must have been for Peter. How they dug into his soul. Possibly Peter was then tempted to say, "Lord, thou art mistaken. I will go to death with Thee, if need be." How little Peter knew then that a few hours later, with deepest remorse and inward shame, he would deny Christ.

The calm, quiet John made no such protestations; but he followed his Lord not only to the judgment hall, but also to the cross. Those who are loudest in the acclaim of their friendship are sometimes first to forsake one in the hour of need, while those who are slow to state their affection are still around when one needs friends most.

Loyalty to a person or a cause often suffers a dreadful shock when that person or cause suddenly becomes unpopular. One must strike a new emotional balance and master his emotions suddenly, or must reassess the person or cause to decide whether to continue his loyalty.

Another factor about loyalty in a crisis is that those who are first to proclaim their loyalty are generally of a greater emotional elasticity. Sometimes one who is emotionally very stable is none the less capable of great depths of depression and heights of elation. In such a person, the reaction is much swifter and more severe, and requires longer to strike the new emotional balance. Peter was such a person as this.

Suppose a friend whom you trusted for years is suddenly placed in most embarrassing circumstances. The evidence looks as if he is guilty as accused. While you are trying to decide what to believe, your emotional balance may be off center, but your loyalty is not necessarily gone. In such a moment you could make a statement you would regret for life. This may have been Peter's case. Possibly one reason he did not go with John to the cross after his remorseful repentance, following his denial of Christ, was that his shame to face Him again was too great.

Another serious consideration is that Peter had a spiritual weakness to combat. His boastful over-confidence sprang from a heart-lack. John, being well known by the officials, went with Christ to the cross, but he also betrayed a spiritual weakness. He wanted to "call fire down from heaven" and burn up the Samaritans who did not wish Christ to pass through their village. His bigotry, pride, anger, and impatience needed Pentecost's fulness just as much as Peter's boastfulness and cowardness.

QUESTION 32

A Question of Perplexity

"Do ye enquire among yourselves of that I said, A little while and ye shall not see me: and again, a little while, and ye shall see me?" John 16:19.

It seems that there had come a few minutes' "break" in the long discourse of the evening (John 13-17), and the disciples were now discussing some things Christ had said. They could never quite comprehend their Master. He was always saying things at which they balked, either because they could not believe them, or did not understand them. They were therefore constantly going back to Him for explanations, or reasoning among themselves as to what He had meant.

On this occasion they were discussing His statement, "A little while, and ye shall not see me, and again, a little while and ye shall see me." This was a riddle to them. The idea of His absence during His time in the grave and His reappearance had never dawned upon them, though He had made it very plain to them that He would rise again after three days.

While they were discussing this, Jesus seems to have called them. The break period was over. They were again in discussion session just before His great prayer for them. He looked at them in tender compassion and asked the question for discussion here. Then He explained to them that He was going away into heaven after His resurrection, but that He would send the Holy Spirit to be their abiding Comforter and Leader. He would take Christ's place, and bring all things He had taught them to their memory. And this, He explained, would be much better than if He remained here in person. For when the Holy Spirit came, He would take of the things of Christ and show them to all men who would believe in Jesus.

His great work then could become universal, and all men could have the opportunity, through the work of the Holy Spirit, to share Christ. This is the essence of His explanation to them that lonely night when His going away seemed to dull all things for them.

QUESTION 33

A Question of Desire

"What will ye that I should do unto you?" Matthew 20:32.

The setting of this question is the healing of the two blind men recorded by Matthew. This story is also recorded by Mark (10:46 ff.) and Luke (18:35 ff.). In the accounts of Mark and Luke, however, there is but one blind man mentioned, and he is named by Mark; whereas, Matthew refers to two but neither one is named. Doubtless, this is the same story in all three instances. All have the same settings, and much the same wording, except that Mark gives his name as *Bartimaeus*. Likely, Mark and Luke single out Bartimaeus as the better known of the two. Mark cites his father's name, which may indicate that his father also was a well known man. It is probably, though not stated, that the more important one of them became a disciple of Christ—one of the hundreds of unnamed followers of Christ in those days. It is said of him that as soon as he received his sight, he "followed Jesus in the way" (Mark 10:52).

At the heart of this story is the Master's searching question, "What will ye that I should do unto you?" Note that Christ asks for *specific* information. In modern language, He asked, "What do you wish Me to do for you?" One can ask God for mercy in general terms all day and *receive nothing*! Christ wishes us to be positive. The man *confessed* his *blindness* in asking for its removal. We must confess our sins if they are to be forgiven (Prov. 28:13; I John 1:9), and to be given the Holy Spirit in our hearts (Luke 11:13).

The story opens with the poor blind beggar sitting by the wayside, crying to Christ for mercy. This blind man was *depressed* because of his physical handicap—*blindness*. Blind people were looked upon as social outcasts. It was thought that they or their parents had "sinned" to cause the blindness. He was *discouraged* by the very people who could most have helped him. The multitude had seen Christ perform many other miracles, and were physically able to have assisted him in getting to Jesus. Instead, "many charged him that he should hold his peace."

Despite all this, he became *desperate* and cried out for help. Here five R's come into play. He *Realized* his need; *Relied* upon the proper source for aid—Jesus; *Raised* his voice for help; *Reached* a climax in his pleading—"and Jesus stood"; *Received* an answer—Jesus "commanded him to be called."

Then comes *Disassociation*—"casting away his garment." What a momentous act of faith in Christ! Before he reached the Master or felt His touch, he cast away his beggar's cloak as something he would *never need again*. Further, this garment was something which might impede his progress toward Christ. So, it must go. As with us—garments of doubt, sin, evil habits and sinful companions, and whatever hinders our progress toward Christ, *must go!*

He was *Determined*—"arose." He stood up; minded not the many hindrances; mustered up the courage, and made his way forward to Christ.

Then comes Destination—"came to Jesus." It is too bad that many never get through the maze of church rituals, sacraments, church membership, good as all these are, and get to *Jesus! This* is the need of the world and the Church today—to *come to Jesus Christ*, past all things that surround Him!

Now, the final word, *Demonstration.* Nothing is said about him shouting or making a physical demonstration, although he most certainly did praise God (See Luke 18:43). The most significant statement about him is that "he followed Jesus in the way." This is the supreme demonstration which the world needs to see in Christians today—a life of Christ, lived out in daily practice.

QUESTION 34

A Question of Husbandry

*"Do men gather grapes of thorns, or figs of thistles?"
Matthew 7:16.*

Couched in the famous "Sermon on the Mount" is this question. Along with this, Christ also reminded His audience that "a good tree cannot bring forth evil fruit, neither can a corrupt tree bring forth good fruit."

In the Scriptures, and in Jewish phraseology, "fruits" are taken to represent any kind of works. "A man's works," says an old writer, "are the *tongue* of his heart, and tell honestly whether he is inwardly corrupt or pure."

Jesus took a horticultural fact that trees can only produce after their kind, and used it to illustrate an equal spiritual truth—that men can only produce lives according to their hearts. The art of "grafting" various types of trees was well known, as Paul's reference certainly shows (Rom. 11:17-21). But this in no way changes the fact that trees essentially produce just what they are. Sinners by nature produce sinning lives. The children of God likewise, having been changed by a miracle of grace, no more love sinful ways. They are now made after the "image of him who hath called them" unto eternal life, and they love His way of life.

Note several things of interest about fruit trees:

1. They require culture. Just as vegetables must be cultivated, so also must fruit trees. Trees need to be plowed and cultivated just as does corn.

Christians, likewise, must have the constant care of spiritual culture. Growth in grace comes by prayer, Bible reading, attending Christian worship services, and other things which help one to grow spiritually. We are "saved by grace," not by works, but these things are not *works* for *salvation*. They are *activities of the love of God* in the heart and life. If we love someone, we show it by our actions toward them.

2. Fruit trees also need *spraying* to kill insects which molest and hurt the fruit. Christians, too, need the Word of God filling their hearts and minds at all times. The things of the world tend to make their fruit faulty. God's Word is a powerful repellent for everything which is not helpful in the Christian life.

3. Fruit trees require *pruning*. Jesus states this in His famous Vine and Branches discourse (John 15). Small growths on the trees, or grape vines act as "suckers" and drain away vital sap which should go into the fruit. If these are allowed to grow, they will in time take the place of the fruit, leaving the tree with only small knotty fruit, or small sour grapes. How much the heavenly Pruner, the Holy Spirit, needs to prune away from the lives of many Christians! This pruning process does not stop with any degree or depth of grace, but continues on as long as one lives. This is why the Christian needs the constantly abiding presence of the Holy Spirit to culture, develop, repel, prune and protect the divine fruit of spiritual life.

QUESTION 35

A Question of Numbers

"Were there not ten cleansed? but where are the nine?" Luke 17:17.

Christ left Samaria and entered into Judea journeying toward Jerusalem, apparently finishing that trip which had taken Him originally into Samaria. It was on the first part of this trip that He had stopped at Sychar and delivered the famous discourse to the woman at the well (John 4). Now He appears to be completing this trip to Jerusalem.

It seems He had just entered a Galilean village when he was met by ten lepers who begged Him to heal them. They had doubtless either seen Him perform miracles, or heard of His mighty works. They knew from all they had heard that He could heal them and make tha well again. When they knew Jesus was passing by, they cried to Him for mercy and help.

Their prayers prevailed. Christ called them to Him and told them what to do to be healed. Note this:

1. They were *not healed* by an instantaneous touch, as some others had been. Our Lord gives no reason for His delayed action in this case. It may have been to teach all men the lesson of absolute faith in Him. They went toward the priest in *faith* and *obedience* to His word. "And as they went, they were healed."

2. God demands faith for anything which we are to receive from Him in the realm of faith. Salvation is by faith. Someone has well said, "He who will not believe till he receives what *he* calls a *reason for it,* is never likely to get his soul saved." God's order is, "He that *believeth* . . . shall be saved." Scripture nowhere stresses *feelings* relative to salvation. Even the "witness of the Spirit" comes *after* believing, or as one is believing.

3. This kind of faith is highly honored of God and He makes it the instrument of numerous miracles. More people need to trust God and not wait for some feeling. When one truly trusts Him, he receives the answer. Plenty of feelings will likely come as a result, then or later.

4. Christ told them to go to the priest and offer the Mosaic requirements under such conditions. He here honors the law. He had not yet fulfilled all the law, until His death, and therefore honors that part which was still in force. This was a ceremonial law and had nothing to do with either salvation or healing. It was simply a basic safety precaution for the priest to make sure, as a doctor would, that the disease was healed, and therefore not in danger of spreading, for leprosy was very cantagious.

When they saw they were healed, one of the ten returned to praise the Lord for His marvelous mercy. Then Jesus asked, "Were there not ten cleansed? but where are the nine?" Christ was apparently disappointed that the nine had not returned with this Samaritan. He showed true gratitude; the others were so busy with matters of ceremony they overlooked the most important thing.

It may be argued that the nine did as they were bidden. Were they not then obeying Him? True, but they could have *returned* to give Him thanks *before* they went on to the priest, or surely afterward. They had evidently either been so full of joy and wished to get the priest's sanction on the miracle at once that they overlooked this important matter; or else, like so many today, they took Christ's healing *for granted* as part of His general goodness, thinking they need not return to express thanks to Him. How often we seem to act like this. "God knows we are grateful," we say to ourselves, "then why be *praising Him all the time?*"

QUESTION 36

A Question of Acquaintance

"Have I been so long time with you, and yet hast thou not known me, Philip? he that hath seen me hath seen the Father; and how sayest thou then, Show us the Father?" John 14:9.

In the last discourse of Jesus (John 13-17), He talked to His disciples about His going to be with the Father, and promised to come again for those who were trusting in Him. He also stated that He was the "way to God." He explained that He was from the Father, was returning to the Father, and that if the disciples had seen Him, truly, then they had seen the Father. Philip stopped Him short with a request: "Lord, show us the Father, and it sufficeth us" (John 14:8). Turning to him, Jesus asked the question at the chapter heading.

In reality, Christ did not rebuke Philip. This request on the part of James, John or Peter, would have been almost inexcusable, for they had seen the glory of Christ and of God in the transfiguration (Matt. 17), and could say, truly, that they had seen the manifestation of the Father's glory. Maybe this was behind Philip's thinking. He, too, as an apostle, wished to see the glory of the Father manifested.

This request was similar to that of Moses (Exod. 33:18), when he asked to see the glory of God. God had shown manifestations of His glory at the giving of the law, and at other times in Jewish history. Christ was instituting a new way to God through His redemptive work. Perhaps Philip wished to see further divine credentials for this great work. He was unaware that Christ was God, manifested in the flesh. Pernaps this was best for the apostles then. Had they fully recognized the Deity of Christ, probably they could never have fellowshiped with Him as they did. It would have kept them in fear every moment. He revealed this truth to them as they were able to receive and accept it, and to live with Him, after its awe-inspiring revelation.

Ministers are sometimes prone to think that if Christ were *actually* in the audience they could preach better. If Christ in all His unveiled glory sat before one while he tried to proclaim His message, how frightening this would be! It is doubtful that one could preach at all, being overcome with his own weakness and inadequacy to proclaim His Word. Yet, no true minister wishes to proclaim His Word without His *veiled Presence* in the power of the Holy Spirit in every ministration.

Christ makes forever plain His declaration of Himself as the Son of God. "God," He had told them, "and I are one; he who has truly seen Me, has seen God, for I am like Him, and He is like me," to paraphrase His words. This likeness was not a physical resemblance. Christ taught that "God is a spirit: and they that worship him must worship him in spirit and in truth" (John 4:24). Christ was like God, then, in spiritual matters. Both hated sin and loved righteousness; both loved mankind and yearned to redeem him; both worked together, and the like. The miracles were the power of God through Christ, and the truth taught was God's truth revealed by Christ.

To see a complete picture of the likeness of God, read the New Testament with fresh vision and new approach, looking for the likeness of God in moral and spiritual ways. Etched upon these pages is the image of the invisible God, as portrayed in Christ's like, acts, doctrine, principles, and spirit. It cannot be otherwise for Christ came to manifest God to mankind.

QUESTION 37

A Question of Faithfulness

"Who then is a faithful and wise servant, whom his lord hath made ruler over his household, to give them meat in due season?" Matthew 24:45.

This question comes in the midst of Christ's discourse about "last things" and His return to earth. Along with His prophecies of His return was His prophecy of the destruction of the temple and the terrible suffering of the Jewish people during that period of tribulation.

Among those somber last words of warning Christ asked the question at the heading. Josephus, learned Jewish historian of a little later time, has recorded for us their complete fulfillment.

Christ prophesied the destruction of Herod's temple, which took 46 years to build. Ancient Jews claimed that this temple was made of white and green spotted marble stones, some of them fifty feet long, twenty-four feet wide and sixteen feet thick. How they were erected remains a mystery. Jesus said, "There shall not be left here one stone upon another that shall not be thrown down."

Christ also warned the Christians to "flee to the mountains" when they saw Jerusalem in military encampment. It is reported that when Titus, the Roman general, threw Jerusalem under siege in 70 A.D., the Christians fled to the mountains. Many of them stayed in the now famous "red city" of Petra, in the mountains of Edom, the country formerly occupied by Esau's descendants. There was once a strong ancient city there.

The buildings were hallowed out of the sides of the red stone mountains in huge caves. These caves were used for homes, stores, shops and other purposes. The Christians occupied them in their distress and were saved from the storm of persecution which destroyed about a million unbelieving Jews which clung to their city to the last. About a million more were sold into slavery.

In this manner, Christ's very words were fulfilled. Titus gave orders to spare the temple in Jerusalem. The Jews, knowing this, took refuge in the temple. The soldiers shot fiery darts into it to roust them out, setting it on fire. So it burned to the ground. When the final blast came, the very walls of the temple were dug up, it is reported, by Roman soldiers in search for gold which they imagined the Jews had stored under them.

Christ intended to impress upon His followers the absolute necessity of faithfulness to their duties. He had just pointed out the terrible fate which awaited those who rejected Him and the folly of trying to withstand the storm when it broke. Now, to paraphrase, He is saying, "Despite all this, let none of these things hinder you from carrying out your duties as servants of God. Allow nothing to so frustrate your mind or upset you emotionally that you will neglect your plain duty."

In these days we need the same exhortation. Some rationalize, "Universal destruction could come upon the world. Therefore, let us have a good time today; it may be later than you think!"

Those who listen to this will soon find themselves morally and spiritually bankrupt. This is not God's way. Do not take it; you will regret it forever. Be faithful to right—it will triumph in the end, and you will then be on the right side.

QUESTION 38

A Question of Trouble

"Why trouble ye the woman?" Matthew 26:10.

Just before His crucifixion, Jesus was entertained in Bethany in the home of "Simon, the leper"—possibly a person whom Christ had healed.

While being entertained, a woman came in with a box of very precious ointment and poured it upon His head. A stream of protest arose from the mercenary-minded disciples about the waste of this very costly perfume. The amount she used was worth a considerable amount of money.

The cruel remarks of the disciples perhaps hurt the woman very deeply. She had done this with the most tender affection, thinking in terms of Christ's death and burial. The disciples, still incased in their shell of materialistic outlook, thought only of financial values.

The Greek for, "Why trouble ye the woman?" may also be rendered, "Why do you put the woman to pain?" In other words, "Why do you pain her heart with your selfish thoughtlessness?"

Sensing the situation, Jesus asked the thoughtless disciples, "Why trouble ye the woman?" To paraphrase His words, He said, "Why do you put her to pain, not detecting her purpose? She came to anoint My body for My burial, being more thoughtful than you. You have the poor with you always, but you will not always have Me with you. It seems you could be a little more thoughtful and have a bit more gratitude. Because of this woman's thoughttulness and love for me, this that she has done will be told for a memorial of her in all the world wherever the Gospel is preached." His words stung them deeply, and rightly so.

How often the Lord is robbed of that which belongs to Him in money, time, and in other things. Some drop a dime in the hat of a poor beggar, or give a quarter to the Salvation Army at Christmas time and think they have done God a great favor! What hypocrisy and sham! Others claim income tax deductions allowable for giving to Church and charity when they have not given a mite. This is cheating, lying and stealing, and will be visited with the burning wrath of God upon those who do it unless they repent.

If all the people who have lied and stolen in this manner would *repent and pay up*, Uncle Sam would have millions of dollars of "conscience money" on his hands! The government has been "forced" to demand receipts for such claimed deductions in many instances. What frightful things the Judgment Day will uncover. How the wicked will gnaw their tongues in eternal pain for their lying hypocrisy! How true was the cry of an ancient heathen at the graveside of one who had been murdered for his wealth: "O! cursed lust of gold! what wilt thou not compel the human heart to perpetrate?"

Be careful what you say about one who has done his best for another. Though the ministry of it may be poor in your sight, it may have been his best—yea, even his all.

QUESTION 39

A Question of Lacking

"When I sent you without purse, and scrip, and shoes, lacked ye anything? And they said, Nothing" Luke 22:35.

Just before the crucifixion Christ gave His disciples some last minute instructions about their work after His final departure for heaven.

In this discourse He asked them about a special experiment they tried out earlier when sending them out two by two (See Luke 10), giving them power to heal the sick, cast out demons and raise the dead. Now, calling this experience to mind, He asked them the question at the heading.

This had been a special mission to test their faith and demonstrate His ability to supply their needs. He explained that when they went on the mission of evangelizing the world after His departure, they should take their purses, scrips, and if they had no swords, buy some for protection.

At first this sounds like strange language from our Lord. But the whole passage may be interpreted as the following paraphrase: "When I sent you on that short journey for a few days (Luke 10), you had little need of money, or staff. But as you go into all the world, you will be traveling in countries which may not be hospitable to you. You will therefore need extra money and clothes. You may even need to look out for your own protection; so, prepare the best you can for this work."

Some scholars think the word "sword" is an *interpolation* added to the original text. If used at all, it may have meant to sell the sword and buy other things. The Greek verb used may lend itself to this interpretation by making it *recessive* to the things to be bought. However, others feel that the word was used here in the *figurative* sense only—that they must look out for their own safety and welfare, when persecuted by others.

God is able and willing to supply our needs if we trust in Him. But if this is pressed too far, it loses its meaning as to God's work. It would be ridiculous for the Standard Oil Company, for instance, to send a man out to work for them, expecting him to make his own way, financially. God does not do business this way, either.

God has called certain ones to give their full time and talent to His cause in spreading the Gospel. It is too bad that many so called have to make a share of their own way in this calling. It is not disgraceful. St. Paul was a tent-maker. William Carey, India's first great modern missionary, made his own way, and that of his missionaries, putting back into God's work tens of thousands of dollars. But these are exceptions, not the rule.

It has often been proved by divinely called workers that God's supply line reaches just as far as the ability of the worker to live a trustful and dependent life in Christ. No worker has ever starved to death on the field under normal conditions. Philippians 4:19 has been a faith-stake to which many a worker has successfully fastened his hope. But Christians should support the workers God has called into His vineyard.

QUESTION 40

A Question of Escape

"Ye serpents, ye generation of vipers, how can ye escape the damnation of hell?" Matthew 23:33.

This question is listed among the several burning words of exhortation, censure and warning which Christ gave in His famous last discourse as recorded by Matthew (Matt. 22-25). This discourse was given in Jerusalem, possibly on the temple grounds to the throngs who had gathered there for the great passover. It was given before the final discourse recorded by John, on the passover night (John 13-17).

The first part of the discourse was given in parables and instructions for His disciples and the multitude. The last part deals with the eschatology of the last days, both of the Jewish age and its frightful end under the Romans (70 A.D.), and of the Christian age, and Christ's return to earth. The middle section of the discourse is given to warnings of the Jews of their sinfulness and blindness, and of the danger in which they stood to lose not only their land, but their souls in perdition if they did not repent and accept Christ as their true Messiah.

In this middle section is the question at the heading, which Christ asked of the Jewish leaders. This must have been a very stark and personally humiliating question. It likely burned into their consciences like liquid fire, arousing whatever last remains of sin-consciousness they had left, and pointing them to God's justice. For those who had passed redemption's point, as it seems some had, it served only to goad them on to secure His death as soon as possible. They never attempted an answer to this question, and were probably not capable of answering it. To answer it properly would have been to confess their sins, and the wrongness of their opposition toward Him. This they were not prepared to do. Like Pilate, they defended their deeds, but never confessed the wrong of their ways.

Many people today recognize their wrong. Conscience has been faithful to them, and the Holy Spirit has warned and striven with them; but like the Pharisees of that day, they will likely never confess their wrongs nor correct them. They will die in their sins, holding their tongues without confession until they are forever silenced in death.

How shall we escape the damnation of hell? There is but one way—through repentance, confession of sin, and faith in Jesus Christ as Saviour. This was what had blocked the Jews. Christ had brought them by His teachings and miracles to the point of decision. They must now either accept Him as the Son of God—their Messiah—or else, reject Him. There could be no neutral grounds. Christ had given them time to decide, and to be convinced of His Sonship, just as God gives youth time in which to come to see their responsibility toward God.

They had had this total opportunity; the light of God had shined into their minds and hearts. They had seen, and were no longer blind. He told them inasmuch as ye say, "we see, therefore, your sin remaineth." They had been convinced, but were unwilling to accept the claims of Christ and allow Him to become their Lord and Master.

This happens when people are exposed to the light of the Gospel of Christ. Soon each one comes to see for himself that Jesus Christ is God's Son, that he owes allegiance to Him as Saviour and Lord. If he accepts this, salvation comes into his heart and he becomes one of God's redeemed children. But if one sees this and thinks the price too great to pay for salvation, then he is in the same position as these ancient Christ-rejecters. He has no hope for heaven, unless he will repent and turn to Christ, for He is the only "escape" from damnation.

QUESTION 41

A Question of Inquisitiveness

"Lovest thou me?" John 21:16.

Peter and six of his friends had gone back to Galilee from Jerusalem after the resurrection of Christ. Christ had promised the disciples, through a message sent by the women, that He would see them in Galilee (Matt. 28:7).

Whether or not Peter and his friends had gone there expecting to see Jesus may never be known, but however that may be, Jesus was there ready to reveal Himself to them. Peter and the group, having fished all night without a catch, were very tired when they spotted someone on the shore. Only after His advice to cast the net to the right of the boat and find a catch, had been successfully carried out did they recognize their advisor as Christ.

Coming to land they found a meal of fish and bread upon the fire. This was evidently a miracle of Christ, for the disciples had caught no fish. "Come and dine," Jesus invited. The word "dine" is from a Greek word which can also be used for *breakfast,* and was so used by Homer, Xenophone and Plutarch. "Come to breakfast," He said to them, literally. The words, "So when they had dined," evidently mean to indicate that Jesus ate with them as He had done before, and showed again His complete power over all forms of nature.

Jesus had some special questions to ask of Peter at this time. Now we shall deal with the implications of the total set of questions, and the last one in particular. In the first question— that of comparison, "Lovest thou me more than these?" the word "love" comes from the Greek *agapa,* generally used to signify *divine love.* This is love on the highest possible level, and means to love *affectionately, supremely, and perfectly.*

To this question Peter made a very cautious reply, "Thou knowest that I love thee." There is none of the old spirit of boastfulness, as before the crucifixion when he boasted, "If all men forsake thee, yet will not I." Bitter experience had humbled and somewhat refined him. Besides, he now saw Christ as the divine Saviour and spoke with subdued humility.

Gazing steadily at him, Jesus asked again, "Lovest thou me?" (v. 16). This is the question of real *inquisitiveness*. Here our Lord changed words, and used the less powerful word, *philos*, indicating *friendship love*. Peter was grieved deeply. Possibly he feared that Christ saw something in his heart which may cause him to *fall again*. More likely he was grieved because Christ used the less meaningful word, *philos*. He first asked, "Do you love Me supremely, with all your heart?" then, switched and said, "Do you even have *esteem*, or *friendship love* for Me?" Each time He assigned to Peter a lower, or less love.

Perhaps this was Christ's way of reminding Peter of his fearful failure. And since Peter was to be raised to such prominence in the Church, his faith and motives must be tested to the last point of stress and strain. But through it all, Peter did not swerve this time. His lesson was well learned, his spirit humbled and his heart proved. He could now look into the eyes of his divine Lord, knowing that He knew him fully, and could say, truly, "Lord, thou knowest all things; thou knowest that I love thee."

In his reply, Peter used the term *philos*, possibly fearing to profess that higher love, after such a fearful failure to manifest it. But the third time, though he still uses *philos*—"friendship love and esteem"—he reinforces it with these declarative words, "Thou *knowest* that I *love* thee." He could not yet say, as he certainly could after Pentecost when his heart was overflowing with a new sense of *agape* love—perfect love—"I have whole, supreme, perfect love for Thee." But he could most solemnly affirm that he now had that loving friendship esteem which would keep him ever following on to know Christ better and finally, to love Him to perfection.

Perfect love to God through Christ is the highest experience in religion. It is the state for which all Christians should ardently seek until they have found it in Christ. It was John Wesley who warned that if one seeks anything more than perfect love, he seeks amiss. No experiences of any kind, whatsoever, can equal this crown of all perfection in religion—perfect love for God and for mankind.

Question 42

A Question of Finding

"What man of you, having an hundred sheep, if he lose one of them, doth not leave the ninety and nine in the wilderness, and go after that which is lost, until he find it?" Luke 15:4.

This question was asked by Christ in connection with His discourse on the Lost and Found things, illustrating God's love and mercy to lost sinners. It is a most encouraging passage for sinners, showing God's love and how He yearns to save the lost.

Possibly the discourse was drawn out partly by the accusations of the scribes and Pharisees that Christ received and entertained sinners. Because He ate with the publicans and sinners, He was called a "glutton and a winebibber."

When they accused Him of eating and mixing with sinners, Jesus told some stories which illustrated *why* He did so. In the first place He asked the question at the heading above. He followed this with the story about the woman and the lost coin. (Luke 15:8).

These two illustrations were followed by one of the most famous stories in any language—the story of the Prodigal Son (Luke 15:11-32), climaxing the illustrations of God's love and willingness to save mankind.

Jesus was a great story-teller. His stories, taken from scenes and situations of everyday life, have become immortal. After all the centuries, His stories are still the most popular and colorful in any language. They are immortal because of the universal messages of love, God's goodness and care with which they are freighted.

The *lost sheep* is the emblem of the lost sinner, or the believer who has wandered away from his Master. No creature strays more easily than a sheep, is more heedless of its way, nor seems less capable of finding its way back to the fold without aid. It is less defenseless and helpless against other beasts. All this is true also of the sinner. But the Good Shepherd is always near to rescue those who will follow. He will take him back to the fold, but only if he can be persuaded by love and tender care to go back, assisted by God's grace.

The same principle may be applied to the money, though here the symbol changes slightly. Money cannot notify one where it is, as the sheep can by his bleating. Money, when lost, is even more hopeless of being found. The *longer it is lost,* the *less probability* there is that it will *ever* be found. It tends to *take on* the *color* of its *surroundings;* hence is even more difficult to locate and becomes covered with *dust* and *dirt.*

The woman in this parable may represent the Church, searching for the lost. The candle of God's Word must be ever burning and the broom of the gospel preaching must be diligently applied, if the lost coins of souls are to be found.

In each case, Christ said there was great rejoicing when the lost was found, explaining that the angels in heaven rejoice when a sinner repents and turns to God.

QUESTION 43

A Question of Weeping

"Woman, why weepest thou?" John 20:15.

Among the tender and heart-warming stories of the resurrection is the one about Mary Magdalene. She was not content to return home as the other ladies did after the angels had assured them that Christ was alive. Instead, she wandered about the garden, doubtless still sobbing out her broken heart. Angels had said He was alive and would see them again. This was enough for the other women, but hardly for Mary.

Suddenly, she saw a man at some distance, but being grief-stricken she paid little attention who it may be. Then she heard the question, "Woman, why weepest thou?" Still downcast, she asked, "Sir, if thou hast borne him hence, tell me where thou hast laid him, and I will take him away." She thought the man was the gardener. Not looking up, she had not seen Him. By *looking down* in our attitudes of despair and doubt, we lose much in life. Much sorrow might be avoided, if we but *looked up* even in the midst of our troubles.

Jesus called, "Mary." The word brought her face up instantly. The old familiar ring of cordiality was now touched with infinite pathos. Quick as a flash she recognized Him and cried, "Master!" She much have rushed toward Him, for He warned her, "Touch me not; for I am not yet ascended to my Father." Then He commissioned her to notify His disciples of His ascension.

By her undying devotion, Mary saw Christ first after His resurrection; and she bore His first post-resurrection message to His disciples. Later, several of the women saw Him, and came and took Him by the feet (Matt. 28:10), *after* Mary saw Him. Evidently between His appearance to Mary and that to the women, He had ascended to heaven and applied His blood upon the Mercy Seat, becoming the approachable Intercessor, the Mediator, to whom all may now come. He invited the disciples to handle Him in later appearances; so evidently He saw Mary even before He had ascended to heaven and completed His mediatorial work,

What high honor and holy privileges come to those who keep close to God! Had Mary been content to leave with the others, this most thrilling story would have been forever absent from the Gospels. Those who have been devoted to God have left the most lasting influence upon the Chruch and the world,

To the womanhood of this world, filled with sorrow, foreboding, and ten thousand cares, Christ is still saying, "Woman, why weepest thou?" What sorrows could be avoided, pains and heartbreak missed, and what glorious hours of happiness and usefulness could be enjoyed if womanhood would only heed that gentle voice! It is an invitation to peace and certainty, to bring all her sins and sorrows, fears and problems, and rest them at the feet of Jesus,

QUESTION 44

A Question of Suffering

"Ought not Christ to have suffered these things, and to enter into his glory?" Luke 24:26.

It was the resurrection day. All was confusion and questioning among the disciples. The women had affirmed that Christ was indeed alive. Mary Magdalene reported having seen Him, and gave His message to the disciples, and the message about His ascension (John 20:15-17). The other women reported that they also had seen Him later, and had even held His feet and worshipped Him. He had told them to go and tell the disciples that He would see them in Galilee (Matt. 28:9, 10). Peter and John had been to the garden and examined His tomb, finding it empty and the confused guards gone off to report what had happened. They had been told by the women that Christ was alive, but so far none of the men had seen Him. Doubtless, this seemed a bit odd to them, that not a single one of the eleven apostles had seen Him alive, nor even seen an angel who affirmed that He was. Their faith had, therefore, to be grounded on secondary evidence, or His pre-Calvary promises to rise again. This message had seemingly been lost sight of in their grief and disappointment.

Two disciples, not apostles, decided to go to the little village of Emmaus on the afternoon of the resurrection. On their way a "stranger" overtook them. Mark explained that He appeared to them "in another form" (Mark 16:12). As they walked they discussed the crucifixion happenings. (Jews often spoke of the Law in their journeys to pass time away.) This stranger asked them, "Ought not Christ to have suffered these things, and to enter into his glory?" Then beginning at Moses, He opened from all the Scriptures the things concerning Himself. Later they said, "Did not our hearts burn within while He opened to us the Scriptures by the way. . . ?"

The sufferings of Christ are here made part of the redemptive program by Christ Himself in His explanation of it to these two disciples. One of these men was Cleopas, and the other is supposed by many learned men, both ancient and modern, to have been *Luke* himself. What better choice could the Saviour have made for this revelation? Both were only laymen, Cleopas, a humble, almost unknown one, and Luke, the cultured physician who was to write more of the New Testament than any other man except Paul,

No one knows *why* Christ chose to manifest Himself to the women first. Only after many hours of mental stress and strain and utmost frustration, and after their faith had been tried to the limit, did Christ choose to allow Himself to be seen by the apostles. Again, the apostles were *not* the *first men* to see Him. Perhaps Christ chose to test their faith to its utmost limits before revealing Himself to them, that they might appreciate His resurrection more when it became firmly established in their minds. They were allowed to see just how hopeless would be their case and that of the Christian message if there were no resurrection. In this way they saw the weaknesses and paltriness of themselves, detached from this great miracle of Christ. Without the resurrection, the whole story of the Gospels would soon have died out, unchampioned and unheralded to the world. The resurrection, then, was shown to them as the cornerstone of Christianity, even by so simple an act as Christ's *delay* in revealing Himself to them.

Christianity is a suf fering religion. Its Master gave it to the world through sufferings, and it has never flinched from sufferings. When it has been at its best spiritually has been in its periods of suffering.

QUESTION 45

A Question of Watching

"What, could ye not watch with me one hour?" Matthew 26:40.

The scene of this question is the garden of Gethsemane. The Passover supper had been served, and Christ had instituted the "Lord's Supper." He had completed His last discourse (John 13-16), and had prayed the famous Parting Prayer, or High Priestly Prayer (John 17). He then cautioned His disciples to linger prayerfully there while He went a bit farther into the garden to pray alone.

At the end of the first season of this prayer, Christ came to the forepart of the garden where He found the would-be watching disciples asleep. To Peter, who had so recently boasted that he would go to death for Christ, Jesus said, "What, could ye not watch with me one hour?" Then He added the caution, "Watch and pray that ye enter not into temptation: the spirit indeed is willing, but the flesh is weak" (Matt. 26:40-41). He then returned to His place of prayer and continued praying.

Peter, whose loud boast shamed the rest, perhaps now disturbed them by his *snoring!* It is often harder to tarry and *watch* than to risk one's life in battle. Quiet, watchful prayer is more difficult to accomplish than the noise of a bold testimony.

Despite Christ's exhortation, when He returned to prayer, the disciples again fell asleep. It has been said that persons in deep grief often easily fall asleep. Mothers with very sick children during the night are reported to doze more easily than normal. Indeed, it is said, "He found them sleeping for sorrow" (Luke 22:45).

This last prayer reached such proportions of mental agony that Christ's sweat became as "great drops of blood," It was a mental agony like which there has been none on earth in prayer. (King Charles IX of France, when he saw his folly in ordering the French Massacre and other sins at his death, is reported to have sweat blood in his mental agony.)

Christ sweat blood in agony *for* man's sins; King Charles sweat blood *because* of his awful sins!

What a sad spectacle the sleeping disciples must have been to our Lord when He returned from His final prayer. He had asked them to watch for "one hour," and they had failed Him. What disappointment that His most trusted friends in His deepest hour of sorrow and greatest time of human need, would so neglect Him as to fall asleep! They should have known He was now in the greatest danger of falling into the hands of His enemies!

But is not this the case today? Was there ever a time when the Church was in greater peril, or need of wakeful, watching, praying Christians than now? There has been no time since before the Protestant Reformation when the Church at large was more asleep to the great needs and dangers of the hour than this. The spirit of revival is much needed in Christendom today. Many who profess religion have very little understanding of the needs of this hour spiritually.

QUESTION 46

A Question of Seeing

"Having eyes, see ye not? and having ears, hear ye not? and do ye not remember?" Mark 8:18.

This question was asked by Christ on two very different occasions. The reference in Mark brings the disciples up sharp in His rebuke for their lack of faith.

They had made the trip to Dalmanutha from Christ's last preaching point. At time for the upcoming meal, they realized they had forgotten to bring any bread along on this trip.

Christ was speaking against the evil leaven of the Pharisees and scribes who, by the misinterpretation of doctrine, were poisoning the people's minds. When He again spoke to His disciples, He warned them to "beware of the leaven of the Pharisees . . . and of Herod." The disciples, not getting His real meaning, felt He was reproaching them for having forgotten to bring bread.

He turned to them and asked the question at the heading. To paraphrase, He asked them, "Where, then, is your faith? Do you not use your eyes and ears? Do you not see nor understand, that if it were merely a question of bread, I could provide this easily for thirteen of us, if I could provide it for several thousand?"

The second question arose out of the way in which a certain woman treated Him while He was being entertained in the home of Simon the Pharisee (Luke 7:44). Simon had been neglectful of the Master, not offering Him even the common footwashing courtesies when He entered his house. During the meal, this woman of low morals came and washed His feet with tears and dried them with her hair. Simon thought in his heart, "If this man were the prophet, He would certainly know who this moral wretch is and never allow her to touch Him in this way."

Christ surprised Simon with a story of a creditor whose client owed him a large sum he could not pay. Another fellow owed him only a small amount, but the good creditor forgave both of them outright.

"Now, Simon, which one of these fellows do you suppose loved that creditor the most?" Christ asked.

"Why, the fellow who had the big debt forgiven, I'd think, Master," he replied.

"Right, Simon. When I came into your house, you did not offer Me the common courtesies of a guest; but this woman has washed my feet with her tears and dried them with her hair. *Do you see the great love this woman has for me?* I tell you, Simon, her many sins are all forgiven. Her love has been great becauso she has been forgiven much. Yours is very small and you are very thoughtless because you have not realized how really great the love of God is!"

Question 47

A Question of Execution

"When the lord therefore of the vineyard cometh, what will he do unto those husbandmen?" Matthew 21:40.

Our Lord's story of the vineyard and the wicked husbandmen as told by Matthew and Mark, was a parable directed to the Jewish leaders. Parables were not new to the Jews. Their prophets had dealt in parabolic teachings for centuries. Jesus was therefore well understood when He taught in parables. Sometimes His parables had such deep and hidden meanings that it was difficult for the people to get them at first, but as He unfolded the truth to them, they began more and more to understand His parabolic teachings.

In this parable (Matt. 21:33-46), Christ portrayed the history of Israel briefly until that moment, then passed on into a prophecy of His own treatment at the hands of the Jewish leaders. Briefly outlined, God is the Householder who planted the vineyard. Palestine may be the vineyard. The Householder's family represents the Jewish nation. The husbandmen are the priests and doctors of the law. The fence may stand for the law of divine protection and the tower for the temple, where God's presence was. The Householder's servants, sent to collect revenues, were the prophets sent from God to convince Israel of their responsibility to God. The son, the heir, who came at last, was of course Christ, God's only Son, whom the Householder sent as the final agent for the harvesting of the vineyard. The stoning and killing of the prophets is covered by Christ's reference to how the wicked husbandmen treated the servants. The treatment accorded the heir, by killing and casting him out of the vineyard, was a prophecy of how Christ Himself, the true Heir, would be treated in His attempt to reach and win them to God.

Some have tried to symbolize this parable as dealing with the Church in the ages ahead of Christ's time, but generally without success.

Likely, the parable has its entire meaning for the Jewish leaders of Christ's day, as His application of it to them bears out.

The question heading this chapter takes on a new significance if we think of it in personal terms. What did God do with that rebellious and wicked nation which demanded Christ's execution? He allowed their city to be torn to shreds by Titus, the Roman general, in 70 A.D. A million were sold into slavery over the world, and about a million more perished there by various means. Jerusalem fell into the hands of "others," the Gentiles, for many centuries.

This is a solemn warning to ministers who have been called of God to protect and care for the church of God. What a day of reckoning there will be for those ministers who have betrayed their trust and have allowed the work of God, over which they were placed, to fall into decay for the lack of plain Gospel preaching!

QUESTION 48

A Question of Touch

"Who touched my clothes?" Mark 5:30.

Jesus had been to Gadara and healed the demon possessed man. He had returned to the other side of the Sea of Galilee, and was preaching to a vast multitude. Jairus, the local synagogue ruler, came falling at His feet, begging mercy and healing for his small daughter.

Immediately, Jesus started with him, but the people blocked His way. Among those pressing toward Him was a woman who had been sick for twelve years with some type of abnormal hemorrhage. Some believe this was possibly connected with a malfunction of menustration. This rendered her unclean ceremonially, according to Jewish sanitation laws. She was not to "touch" another person; hence, she desired to touch, not the *person* of Christ, but merely the "hem"—outer fringe of His garment. This blue fringe worn by devout Jews testified to their faith in God. She believed that in doing this she would be healed.

The nature of her illness was chronic. Long affliction had taken what little she had. She could secure no more money for treatment. Her case was hopeless—except for Christ's help.

Just as she was about to reach Him, He was going away. With "fear and trembling," lest her mission even now end in disastrous failure, she pressed her way through the crowd. At last, she touched His garment. Jesus asked, "Who touched my clothes?" He knew that healing power had gone out of Him. Mark's statement that she "felt in her body that she was healed" may be stated even stronger. The Greek here rendered "felt" is actually from the word "knowing," and may read, *"she knew she had been healed."*

QUESTION 49

A Question of Purpose

"And Jesus said unto him, "Friend, wherefore art thou come?" Matthew 26:50.

Jesus stood at the garden gate of Gethsemane. The long prayer vigil of frightful agony was now forever past. The sleeping disciples, who had left Him so alone in His darkest hour, were now thoroughly aroused by the approaching mob. The night was far spent; the morning, a day to be remembered for all time to come, was now dawning.

Other scenes had also been forever fixed. Jewish leaders had finally been able to make a deal with a renegade disciple of the Christ to betray Him. In the flickering lights of the high priest's office, the covetous hand of Judas had reached out its long, bony fingers and clasped 30 pieces of silver in its grasping palm. A call in the night to the captain in charge of troops at the Roman garrison in the city had secured a sufficient number of soldiers to bring back the wanted captive.

With swords, staves, and lanterns the soldiers and Judas made their way down the slopes from Jerusalem across the little brook of Kidron and were now finishing the slow march to the garden of Gethsemane. Stealthily they slipped along until at last they spotted in the moonlight the little knot of men huddled together just inside the garden gate.

The traitorous Judas whispered, "Here is your sign—whomsoever I kiss is the one. Hold Him fast once you have Him." With this they moved onward. The little group of men did not move. The soldiers were amazed. As they approached them, Judas stepped forth swiftly and said, "Hail, Master," and kissed Jesus. Jesus stood as still as a statue. Looking at Judas He asked, "Friend, wherefore art thou come?"

What a tender word, *Friend!* Yet, Jesus knew this was a kiss of betrayal. It seems as if Christ wanted to prove to Judas, once for all, that His love was still warm and unwavering. How low Judas had sunk; and yet, how tender and winsome were these last words of Christ to him! Words of forgiving love, pity and compassion and welcome to return.

How many followers of our Lord have betrayed Him in the ages since Judas' day! Few have done so as openly and as flagrantly as Judas betrayed Him, but many have left His cause in times of greatest need. But Christ still stands ready to pardon and receive back to Himself all who will return, even though they have betrayed Him.

QUESTION 50

A Question of Anxiety

"My God, my God, why hast thou forsaken me?" Matthew 27:46.

This was our Lord's last question before His death. It came from the depth of His soul, with unspeakable deep and sad longings for the manifested favor of God in His darkest hour. It was the climax of the greatest drama in human history. The pathos of this cry has rung down through the corridors of all time.

The words of this question are quoted from Psalm 22:1, the crucifixion Psalm. This Psalm, read carefully in the light of the crucifixion story, seems to state in word pictures and figures of speech almost exactly what the Gospels do in historical records. It is a remarkable testimony to the accuracy of the divine revelation of God. David wrote this psalm almost 1,000 years before Christ, 300 years before the founding of Rome and long before the method of crucifixion was even thought about.

The exact meaning of this question is open to serious discussion. Unbelievers and critics of Christ have said that such a cry from Christ was "unworthy of a man who suffers, conscious of his innocence, and argue imbecility, impatience and despair."

There may be two possible explanations. Critical examination of the textual passages in the originals seems to reveal that the words as we have them may not be the same words as they were spoken by Christ. The translations may be somewhat at fault. Instead of "why hast thou forsaken me?" it may be rendered, *"To what sort of persons hast thou left me?"* or again, *"Why hast thou abandoned me to reproach?"* according to an old Latin version before the days of St. Jerome in the third century.

— 111 —

It is hardly worthy of Christ to have questioned the Father as to *why* He had been called upon to suffer, when He had outlined to His disciples several times *why* He had come to suffer and die for mankind.

The idea that God had "forsaken" Him is hardly in keeping with the truth of the Trinity of God. An expression used in Job 26:11 may fit this description quite well, "God hath turned me over into the hands of the wicked." Perhaps another sense may be, "My God, my God, how astonishing is the wickedness of those into whose hands I am fallen!" The word translated "why" in this passage was often used in the Septuagint version in another sense, as, "to what?" or "to what purpose?"

There is, however, another possible explanation: Christ certainly knew *why* He had come to this hour, and could *not* be *forsaken of God* as commonly understood, since "in him dwelt all the fulness of the Godhead bodily." But Deity might *restrain* so much *consoling support* as to leave the *human nature* most *keenly sensible* of the horrors of carrying the sins of all the world and suffering for them. In this sense, there may have been the proper feeling of *aloneness,* as He "trod the winepress of God alone." While there could never have been complete forsaking, there may have been the feeling of bearing man's sins alone, and this may be the sense in which the question is to be understood.

Whatever the technical explanations, they still leave us face to face with the suffering Christ, alone, in His deepest sorrow for the sins of mankind.

Christians sometimes feel forsaken and *alone* in their sufferings. If God *did not* condemn His Son for His cry of "why?" in His darkest hour, most certainly, He will never condemn one of His suffering children if in his loneliness he cries out, "My God, why. . . ?" Let us, like Christ, commit our souls to a loving and merciful God when we suffer and be assured that as Christ arose from death to life immortal, so we, too, shall triumph in Christ at last.

QUESTION 51

A Question of Likeness

"Whereunto then shall I liken the men of this generation? and to what are they like?" Luke 7:31.

Jesus pronounced John the Baptist one of the greatest men ever born. The common people accepted this accreditation with joy. The leaders, however, rejected this high citation with jealousy and revenge in their hearts. Knowing their wickedness, Jesus rebuked them in scathing language. Then He chided them for being like children, who, when played for would not dance, and when mourned for, would not *weep*—literally—*beat the breast in lamentation*. Possibly Christ referred to well known children's games, ranging from the dance to the funeral mimicry. He reminded them how childish and selfish their inner lives were,

They said John the Baptist deceived the people; and that Christ was a glutton and wine-bibber. John was an ascetic, rarely appearing publicly, except for preaching. Christ was socially prominent, dining with both poor and wealthy. But to these evil minded leaders, neither one was acceptable. One *cannot* please persons whose minds are set *not* to accept him, On the other hand, someone whom they *intend* to honor may be a stupid ox, yet they will laud him as a "great man."

Jesus said on this occasion, "But wisdom is justified of her children." This may better be rendered, "justified of her *works*," according to the very oldest versions. *Wisdom* here may also be an appellation of this divine wisdom by Christ to Himself, meaning that Christ and John were children of the divine wisdom, whose works justified them. Wisdom, in this sense, refers to that divine embodiment as used by the Proverb writer (Proverbs 7), much in the same sense as the term "Word" is used in John 1:1, 2.

The question of *likeness,* then, comes back to this—we are like what we believe and what we practice.

QUESTION 52

A Question of Knowledge

"Art thou a master in Israel, and knowest not these things?" John 3:10.

Various theories as to why Nicodemus came to Christ at *night* have been offered: he was busy during the day; he recognized Christ was busy during the day; he was ashamed, as a leader, to be seen talking with Jesus; and he was afraid of the Jews.

Doubtless, "fear of the Jews" was the major reason. Christ went right to the heart of the matter, outlining for Nicodemus the only way to become acquainted with God.

The discussion is most likely given to us only in brief substance by John. Christ opened up a piercing point when He asked Nicodemus the question above.

Some of the basic truths are: Nicodemus side-stepped the issue, glossed it over by questions, or was just plainly ignorant of this great truth. Jesus put the question in a personal, stinging form. In modern language He was saying, "Do you mean you are a minister of the Word of God, and do not know the meaning of this simple truth? All people must be made anew by the Spirit of God, or they can have no part with God."

Christ introduced to Nicodemus the "New Birth." The term, "born again," should be rendered, "born from above." It may likewise be rendered *born anew*. Mankind is born wrong. "In sin did my mother conceive me, and in iniquity was I born," David cried. He must be *born anew, born of God*, to be right with God.

Natural birth gives us human personality; but only the Spirit's rebirth gives us spiritual life and prepares us to communicate with God. Without this rebirth, man's "dead in trespasses and sins" (Eph. 2:1), still a child of the devil, "Ye are of your father the devil . . ." (John 8:44).

Ministers and Sunday school teachers should make clear to young people especially, the *deep need* for being born of God. There is no salvation nor grace from God in natural birth. None who reject God's grace can go to heaven without this change of heart by spiritual re-birth. This truth should be emphasized. The absence of this element from preaching is killing the Church.

Unless one's religious experience has introduced him to God through faith in Christ, and has taken away his desire for the sinful life and given him a sense of love for God and his fellowman, he has missed the true meaning of the Christian religion.

QUESTION 53

A Question of Words

"But if ye believe not his writings, how shall ye believe my words?" John 5:47.

Jesus lectured to the Jews on His Sonship and deity from His Old Testament credentials, from Moses onward. He explained His and His Father's relationship and asserted His divine prerogative to raise the dead at the last day. He made plain to them His claims, so there may be no mistake about their acceptance or rejection of Him.

He spoke of His *works* and His *words,* as a witness to His deity, and also the work of John the Baptist as His divinely appointed forerunner. Finally, He appealed to the Scriptures (John 5:39) for a witness. It seems that the Jewish leaders were hopelessly blind to all these evidences.

Jesus climaxed His argument with reference to the key figure of all Jewish history, tradition and lore—*Moses.* He told them that even Moses, on whom they so completely depended, had predicted His coming. They had accepted the historical Moses, but his prophetic utterances referring to Christ, they had covered with their own meanings, and rejected Christ's references to them. His final statement to them was our question at the chapter heading.

Here Christ rested His case for divine evidences of His Sonship and deity. Those who say that Jesus Christ never claimed Sonship with God other than as everyone is a son of God, have either glossed over John 5-8, miserably failed to understand the plain language of the New Testament, or are so blinded by preconceived ideas and unbelieving minds, that they cannot see this truth.

QUESTION 54

A Question of Reward

"For if ye love them which love you, what reward have ye? do not even the publicans the same?" Matthew 5:46.

There is much in the New Testament about "rewards." The Old Testament emphasizes punishment for sin, sowing and reaping as an inevitable law and pictures the wrath and justice of God, without much emphasis upon the rewards of the saints.

Jesus placed considerable emphasis upon rewards for kingdom citizenship and work done to forward His cause. He said, a "cup of cold water, if given in the name of a disciple, shall in no case lose its reward."

A glance at this passage (Matt. 5:27-48) shows that the law's requirrnents versus Christ's requirements was a point of interest.

Much of the old law was negative in its approach. It had served to *prohibit*, forbid, condemn, and hold in check the evil propensities of men. It offered fearful punishments for disobedience. God wanted to impress Israel that He meant what He said about the importance of obedience to the law.

Jesus lifted up this collapsing system for a true gospel insight into it. It had served as a "schoolmaster to bring us to Christ." Its work was done. Men were no longer merely to love those who loved them, but to love their *enemies*—a thing rather foreign to Old Testament conduct. The old order was to be *reversed*. Whatever one had *not* done before was now to be *required;* much he had done was no longer needed.

Old Testament economy was largely *ceremonial;* Christ's way of life was to be *spiritual*. Under law, man's weaknesses were overlooked; under grace, they are to be removed by divine regeneration, and he is strengthened to do the will of God.

Summing it up in paraphrase, Christs asks, "If you keep only the practices of the worldlings about you, what reward can you expect? What right have you to expect a heavenly reward if you do not show the fruits of a spiritual life? Do not even the Roman tax collectors, whom the Jews considered as the worst of sinners, have a system of ethics by which they honor those whom they love? If you, then, as a professing Christian show no more love, compassion, and Christlikeness than the rest of the sinners around you, why expect a reward in heaven?"

QUESTION 55

A Question of Dividing

"Man, who made me a judge or a divider over you?" Luke 12:14.

Two brothers had evidently had a squabble over their property rights. They apparently appealed to Jesus for help, After the brother had stated his case, he was quite startled by Jesus pointedly asking him the question above. Jesus then warned him to beware of covetousness and told the "Story of the Rich Fool."

In the light of this story of the uncertainty of riches and the sureness of death, the man probably saw his duty clearly.

Christ has set forth in His Gospel the principles by which mankind should be governed in matters of economics, finances, property rights and matters of morals and ethics.

These two brothers could very quickly have settled the matters of their property division by the simple, unselfish application of the Golden Rule, *"All things, therefore, whatsoever ye would that men should do unto you, do ye even the same unto them."* It is as simple as this—apply the Golden Rule to life's daily practices and you will come out with the correct treatment of everyone else.

QUESTION 56

A Question of the Times

"How is it that ye do not discern this time?" Luke 12:56.
Christ warned the multitude against hypocrisy and worldly cares and spoke of those who would endure unto the end and be among the eternally blessed.

He pointed out that when a cloud rose out of the west, they predicted rain, and it came to pass. A south wind was cause for expecting heat, which generally proved true.

He commended them for their ability to forecast the weather by depending upon natural phenomena, but scathed them for their failure to apply the same common sense interpretation to spiritual things. By understanding the signs of the times, they could have reasoned that it was time for Christ to appear among men. Had they accepted the prophecies as they daily unfolded in the life of Christ, they could not have failed to have recognized His mission and His work. But men who accepted the natural means of interpretating many things would not accept the plainest prophecies nor the strongest credentials which God could have given to Christ, that He was His Son.

Man has read the meteorological signs of his age for centuries; learned the signs of the stars and how to chart his worldwide treks across lands and seas; has mastered science, squeezing from it tightly held secrets enough to unlock the universe at certain points, and to blow it to smithereens with his frightful bombs.

But with all his insight and wisdom, man has never learned to read the "signs of the times," spiritually, nor to read aright his own heart's spiritual needs. The aching void and unsatisfied vacuum within him, he thinks can be filled with material possessions and the realizations of certain ambitions; but these never satisfy. Only in Christ can man be fully satisfied.

QUESTION 57

A Question of Understanding

"Have ye understood all those things?" Matthew 13:51.

Matthew chapter 13 introduces the major parables of the Kingdom of Heaven. Up to this time, Jesus had taught quite largely in plain language, unadorned by many figures of speech.

Chapter 12 records the Jews' rejection of Jesus completely, even accusing Him of devil possession. Upon this charge He delivered His most powerful warning explaining to them that they were guilty of the blasphemy against the Holy Ghost (Matt. 12:31, 32. Read Matt. 12:22-50 for the whole setting of this climactic drama.) (See the author's book, *The Unpardonable Sin Explained*, for a complete explanation of the blasphemy against the Holy Spirit; its dangers, and whether or not it may be committed today, and its results.)

When the Jewish leaders rejected Christ as the Messiah, He then introduced the kingdom of heaven and set forth the idea of the Church and its work and its place in the world.

Jesus gave His disciples and the multitudes the numerous parables about the kingdom of heaven. He finally asked if they "understood all these things." They assured Him they had (Matt. 13:51). Perhaps the disciples were a little hasty in their reply, for later we find them asking Him the meaning of many of these things.

A few facts about parables: Whedon says the purpose of a parable was threefold: "To reveal, to conceal, and to perpetuate. It revealed the sacred truth by the power of anology and illustration. It concealed the truth from him who had not, by proper sympathy or previous instruction, the true key to its hidden meaning. To such a one it was a riddle or a tale. And so our Lord could give to His disciples in this method the deepest secrets of His kingdom for ages, while the caviler who would have abused the truth heard without understanding. (See Matt. 5:11.) But the truth thus embodied in the narrative was, as it were, materialized and made fit for perpetuation."

If one can master his apt definition of a parable, he will be much better prepared to understand much of the teachings of Jesus. Much that He taught was in parables. Among His last words before going to the cross was a parable: "If they do these things in the green tree, what shall be done in the dry?" (Luke 23:31).

Understanding God's Word is important. God's Word is food to the soul, water to the thirsty, light to the pathway, sight to the eyes, wisdom for the prudent, guidance for those who know not the way, and strength for the weak and the weary. It is very needful that it be understood. What company would put out a road map which no one could read or a Book of Rules for its employees which not one of them could understand! God has given us his Word to be our guide and He expects us to understand it for this purpose.

QUESTION 58

A Question of Signs

"Why doth this generation seek after a sign?" Mark 8:12.

Christ had just landed on the coast of Dalmanutha after feeding the four thousand as recorded by Mark. He had hardly gotten ashore when the Pharisees and others began testing Him relative to His prophetic claims. They requested some *sign from heaven* to prove His claims.

It was as if they had said, "We don't believe in Your professed sincerity. We think You are a big *fake*. Now, prove otherwise!" Jesus, deeply grieved that He could do nothing for them, simply said, "There shall no sign be given unto this generation." According to Mark's report, Christ reboarded the little ship and sailed away, leaving them to their unbelieving fate.

On another occasion when Jesus was requested to show the crowd some sign of His power, He said, "Except ye see signs and wonders, ye will not believe." On yet another occasion He cried in grief to His disciples, "O faithless and perverse peneration, how long shall I be with you, how long shall I suffer you?" (Matt. 17:17). Then He healed the lad in their presence. He indicated that had they but *exercised the faith which they had in Him*, He would have healed the lad.

The tragic thing about their unbelief is that after all the signs and wonders Christ wrought, they still would not believe. When Lazarus was raised from the dead, many common people believed end were converted to Christ. But John reports that the leaders planned to even *put Lazarus to death* because his being alive made others believe. Jesus' raising Lazarus did not effect a turn to God and faith in Him in their hearts at all. He came as near to them as He could, but to no avail. Some will not believe no matter *what* the evidence!

Question 59

A Question of What To Say

"And what shall I say?" John 12:27.

The scene of this question is at the tenple in Jerusalem during the feast. The disciples had just presented the Greek inquirers who wished to meet Christ. Jesus told them in a parable that unless a grain of wheat was planted and died, there could be no new life come from it.

Christ prophesied His own death and resurrection in this saying to the Greeks, declaring this was God's way to provide salvation for mankind.

This great truth is an enduring principle of the Christian religion. Not only was He to practice this principle, but it was also to become operative in the lives of His followers. Only as His followers laid down their lives in total dedication and full commitment to Him and became filled with the Holy Spirit in following Him through spiritual death and resurrection could there be any true spiritual life for them.

John relates here that our Lord became "troubled in his spirit." Calvary was just ahead of Him with its most terrifying death.

In His petition to the Father, Christ said, "And what shall I say? Father, save me from this hour: but for this cause came I unto this hour." Closer examination of this passage as it stands makes it sound as if Christ had contradicted Himself. The Greek here could be rendered in a paraphrase, "And why should I say, Father, save me from this hour, when from this cause came I unto this hour?" One will see at a glance that this makes the passage much more easily understood. Perhaps this is the real meaning of the original. It is certainly much more in keeping with the spirit and attitude of Christ toward His death as revealed in other places where He speaks of it.

There is diversity of opinion as to what is meant in Christ's Gethsemane prayer, "Father, let this cup pass from me. . . ." One interpretation is that being human, Christ dreaded the cross and sought to find a way around it. Knowing there was none, He acquiesced in it as the Father's will. This supports the weakness of the flesh in Him, and makes way for His followers to also feel a proper sense of drawing back from any painful experience which they may face even for His sake and the Gospel's.

The more correct view is that Christ here prayed for *strength* to go to the cross that He may not die before He reached it. This is much more in keeping with His other references to His death on the cross. The fact that angels appeared and *strengthened* Him supports this opinion.

QUESTION 60

A Question of Intention

"*Judas, betrayest thou the Son of man with a kiss?*" Luke 22:48.

Judas had done his wretched work quickly and successfully. The mob now arrived at the garden to arrest Christ and lead Him to the chief priests. Christ's agony of prayer ended, He calmly faced His future. Peter and the other disciples, aroused out of slumber, now saw the peril into which they had fallen. The pale moon, sliding down over the cloudless heavens, made the shadows of things look long and foreboding. There was a tenseness that had never been felt before.

Moving closer to the garden scene was a dark figure at the head of a well knotted group of Roman soldiers. Judas had assured them that He would likely be with His disciples alone in the garden about this time. It would be sensible to arrest Him before the masses began stirring.

After entering the garden, there emerged a figure from the shadows into the plain moonlight. Judas recognized Him instantly. Moving quietly up to Him, Judas took His hand in his own traitorous one and planted upon it a kiss of abject and disgraceful betrayal. Jesus looked into Judas' face. The moonbeams must have revealed something of the tenderness of Christ's face. "Judas, betrayest thou the Son of man with a kiss?" That question has rung out through the corridors of all time since. Then Judas retired a bit and said to his conspirators, "This is the man; take Him." Suddenly, the frightfulness of the whole scene dawned upon the rough soldiers and they fell back, almost unable to believe what their eyes had just seen.

Jesus asked simply, "Are ye come out, as against a thief, with swords and staves to take me?" There was no answer. The silence of the night became unbearable. Immediately the captain of the soldiers advanced and placed Jesus under arrest and led Him away.

What a strange circumstance this is. Rough, pagan soldiers leading away to judgment an innocent victim of a murderous plot and a wretched betrayal by His own people. Christ is still most often and most seriously betrayed to the world by His professed followers. No wound is so deep as that cut by a supposed friend.

QUESTION 61

A Question of Placing

"Where have ye laid him?" John 11:34.

When Jesus came to the home of Mary and Martha and found Lazarus dead, He formed this simple question, "Where have ye laid him?"

This query reveals the humanity of Jesus. Even though He told the disciples two days before, miles away, that Lazarus was dead, He needed to be shown his grave.

Christ never does anything for us that we can do for ourselves. Could not One who had power to raise the dead have known where he lay? He did not remove the stone over the door. Christ never seems to have done what His followers had the ability to do for themselves.

Christ is asking His followers today where relatives and friends are. It is *our* responsibility to lead them to Him, and to take Him to them in our prayers. "Where *have ye* laid him?" Do not suppose salvation is all on Christ's part. We must bring sinners to Him by all and every means we can.

The story of Lazarus is replete with many spiritual illustrations. Let us note a few lessons which may be drawn from this story of Lazarus:

1. The story opens with Lazarus as a *sick* man. He was one of Christ's most intimate friends, but he was sick.

Mankind is a sin-sick being. Isaiah describes this sickness (Iea. 1:5-9), and Paul explained this malady as a very serious disorder of man (Rom. 1:17-32).

2. Lazarus became *progressively worse*. Jesus did not come to his aid, but finally prophesied his death. Sin likewise is a malady which grows steadily worse till death (Rom. 6:23).

3. Then, we have Lazarus the *dead man*. Mankind is said to be "dead in trespasses and sins" (Eph. 2:1). Good works mean nothing, any more than taking food to a corpse to revive him. As the creed says, "Man is very far gone from original righteousness...." Ezekiel shouted to Israel, "Turn ye, turn ye, ... for why will ye die, O house of Israel?" and, "The soul that sinneth, it shall die" (Ezek. 33:11; 18:4, 20).

4. Lazarus became the *entombed man*. Sin corrupts man and slays him spiritually, so that he is dead to all that is holy and good. Also it *binds* him in tomb-like deadness. Romans 6 speaks of this bondage of sin and being "servants" to sin.

5. As the story progresses Jesus appears on the scene, and we have Lazarus the *raised man*. He now has life in him again, but is still in grave clothes. Old life attachments need to be removed as the new life in Christ progresses. We are raised to newness of life in Christ as the Scriptures teach in Rom. 6:1-5; and II Cor. 6:17.

6. After Lazarus was alive again, Jesus cried, "Loose him and let him go." The liberty of the children of God is often spoken of in Scripture by symbolism and often by direct reference to freedoms enjoyed by spiritually minded Christians. St. Paul speaks of a liberty for Christians (Rom. 7:24, 26; 8:1-11). There is a liberty in Christ available to His followers by which they may lead a useful and spiritual life.

7. The last scene of Lazarus in the New Testament is when he is *feasting with Jesus* (John 12:1). As far as we know, Lazarus is still feasting with Christ in that "more excellent glory that fadeth not away." One may in this manner trace the life of the sinner from his sickness of sin to his final and glorious association, feasting with Christ forever.

QUESTION 62

A Question of Supposition

"Suppose ye that I am come to give peace on earth? I tell you, Nay; but rather division" Luke 12:51.

It is strikingly strange that the Christ who came to earth to bring "peace on earth, and good will to men," also brought some of earth's most serious divisions. Whole families have been divided by Him, and even nations and civilizations have drawn between them the divisive lines because of this "Christ of peace."

In what sense did He not bring peace, but division? He explained this question (vv. 52 and 53). He brings peace of heart to all who will accept Him, but this very fact often produces division, separation, hard feelings and contention among those who refuse to accept Him. One *cannot* accept Christ's complete Lordship of his life and still live in sin. Christ laid down the eternal ultimatum concerning His way of separation. He said, "No man can serve two masters. . . . He that is not for me is against me, and he that gathereth not with me scattereth abroad." It is impossible to mix righteous living and unholy conduct. One cannot go forward with Christ and hold on to sin in his heart.

When one in the home becomes a true Christian, there is bound to come division, if the other members of the family do not take Christ's way. Certainly, the Christian should cooperate with the non-Christian as far as is possible without defiling his own Christian conscience. But how far may a Christian go in this? Certainly, not so far as to bring condemnation for sin into his life.

Communism and Christianity are in worldwide conflict, for example. Those who imagine that true Christianity and true

Communism can ever be reconciled, show their utter lack of understanding either of them: Each demands the fullest devotion. One demands simple faith in God and a way of Christlikeness, the other, an athestic and a materialistic way of life. Christianity is suited to the nature of man's total needs; Communism is contrary to all his *basic* and *natural* needs. As a bad carbuncle on society, it must perish from the earth forever in course of time. It cannot succeed, for it has inherent in it the seeds of its own destruction!

QUESTION 63

A Question of Sufficiency

"For which of you, intending to build a tower, sitteth not down first, and counteth the cost, whether he have sufficient to finish it?" Luke 14:28.

One day while Jesus was teaching, He made some very challenging statements to the crowd about cross bearing. Luke records that He said if one came to be His follower and did not "hate" his father, mother, and others, he could not be His disciple (Luke 14:26). This sounds very strong, but Matthew 10:37 gives the more accurate meaning, "If any man love father or mother *more* than me. . . ."

The Greek word here rendered "hate" literally means to *have less love*, and not to hate in the ordinary sense of the word. This also applies to the passage in Romans 9:13, "Jacob have I loved, but Esau have I hated." This choice was made before the children were even born, but God is not saying He actually *hated* Esau. He had done nothing unrighteous for which God's wrath could be unleased against him. The real meaning, then, is simply, *Jacob have I loved more, Esau I have loved less.*

This is a memorable question on completing a task begun. If one does not count the cost, he may run into the embarrassing position of starting without finishing and becoming a public laughing stock. There is always a sort of sadness about unfinished buildings. They stand alone, apart, unappreciated, a mark of someone's lack of good sense and judgment.

Life's highway is strewn with the derelicts of life who started but did not finish their course. They are to be found from every walk of life. The great majority of these must be marked up to *unwillingness to pursue to the end the chosen course.*

Saddest of all are multitudes of moral and spiritual derelicts who have failed to "count the cost," and have fallen by the wayside. Multitudes offer reasons why they did not go on in the Christian way, but these are only *excuses* which will not stand the fire of the Judgment. God will accept no excuse for our failure to serve Him. An *excuse* is merely the *skin of a reason, stuffed with a lie!* There is no reason, ever, anywhere, any time, why one should not serve God. So, count the cost and prepare to finish your course for Christ.

QUESTION 64

A Question of Images

"Whose is this image and superscription?" Matthew 22:20.

Determined Jewish leaders were trying to trap Christ in some manner, so they might have an alibi for destroying Him. How strange that since the days of Cain and Abel, the wicked have sought every means to embarrass, discourage, discredit, ridicule, or kill the good people of earth. Goodness has ever trodden the pathway of malignant treatment and persecution in this world.

Christ found no exception to this rule of treatment. His only purpose in coming to earth was to fulfill His Father's will in bringing salvation to all men who would turn to Him. "The Son of man came not to destroy men's lives but to save them."

Clever spies from the Jewish leaders one day asked Christ whether it was right to pay tribute to Caesar. Seeing through their hypocrisy instantly, Christ asked to see the "tribute money." Looking at the coin, He asked, "Whose is this image and superscription?" (Matt. 22:20). When they replied, "Caesar's," He gave them the classic answer of the ages: "Render therefore unto Caesar, the things which are Caesar's: and unto God, the things which are God's." At this reply, they gasped for breath, and left Him without another word. This committee must have had a rather difficult time making a satisfactory report to the leaders!

H. G. Wells, agnostic English historian, in his *Outlines of World History,* remarked that when Christ answered His critics as He did, He well knew that "when men render to God the things that are God's, there will be little left for Ceasar"! Wells here strikes the central note of Christ's message. when God has all there is of a man's life, there will be little left for this world and its affairs.

Christians owe loyalty to their government if it is based upon human rights, human freedoms and divine laws which accord with the Scriptures. But Christians are not obligated to stain their consciences before God by a slavish submission to that which is both unscriptural and contrary to basic human rights of political, moral, social and religious freedoms of the highest nature. Mankind is a free being and no government has the right to restrict his essential liberties in any of these forms. Nor does a man have to obey or honor such a government under these conditions. But good government is essential to man's well being and must be supported and defended by Christians, in all forms.

Question 65

A Question of Comparison

"Simon Peter, son of Jonas, lovest thou me more than these?" John 21:15.

Jesus had revealed Himself to His disciples several times before this seashore scene. His identity was now established beyond any possibility of doubt. This was His seventh appearance after His resurrection. Christ had promised the disciples at the resurrection that He would see them again in Galilee through the message sent by Mary (Matt. 28:7; Mark 16:7). This seems to have been the way in which that promise was fulfilled.

The opening account (John 21:1-3) tells us who was there. Among the six present, three were to become the most famous in the early church—Peter, James and John,

Likely, with heavy hearts and downcast spirits the disciples had returned to take up their lonely vigil that night on Galilee. They were probably in familiar waters where they had gotten good catches before.

As the night wore away, they were weary and possibly somewhat discouraged. Not a fish had been caught. Just as they were heading the boat toward shore, someone caught a glimpse of a figure on the beach. Instantly, the stranger's voice rang out over the waves, "Children, have ye any meat?"

"No," came the plaintive reply.

"Cast the net on the right side of the boat and ye shall find," the voice from the shore said. Hardly had the net dipped into the water until it was filling with fish. By this time Peter and the others recognized Christ. Peter jumped into the water and headed for shore.

After a good breakfast, Jesus turned to Peter and said, "Simon Peter, son of Jonas, lovest thou me more than these?"

To paraphrase it, He said, "Peter, you professed that you loved Me more than these did, and that you would go with Me even to death. Do you still think you love Me more than these other disciples do?"

Peter's modest reply was, "Lord, thou knowest that I love thee." Another explanation is: "Peter, do you love Me more than *these temporal things*—bread and fish—which you are eating?" The first explanation is likely the correct one, although both may be covered in the question.

Peter had denied Christ three times. Now Christ asked him three times to state his love and purpose in his restoration. Those who deny Christ must find means to openly acknowledge Him with as such vigor and earnestness as they denied Him.

QUESTION 66

A Question of Smiting

"Why smitest thou me?" John 18:23.

Jesus was being questioned before the high priest in the early morning hours of His trial. The high priest asked Him about His disciples and doctrine. Jesus reminded him that he knew what He had said and of His disciples. A cocky little officer rebuked Christ and smote Him with the palm of his hand, because He had answered the high priest in a forthright manner.

Turning to the little wart, the Saviour said in simple, dignified words, doubtless with burning eyes of penetration, "If I have spoken evil, bear witness of the evil: but if well, why smitest thou me?" At these words the little officer evidently withered away and dried up for good! Possibly those penetrating eyes burned through his shriveled little soul, until he wanted nothing more to do with this strange Man! Nothing more is ever recorded of him,

Christ was never once trapped by anyone. He knew men and was never their victim, although they often found themselves His victims, in mighty, vice-gripping situations.

Sometimes, as before Pilate, Christ's *silences* could be equally as terrifying as His words. Pilate must have withered and sweat under these. On one occasion he was so stunned that he shouted to Christ, "Dost thou not know that I have power to crucify thee, or to release thee!" Jesus was not the least disturbed. Looking at Pilate with those eyes which wicked men always tried to avoid, He replied in perfect calmness, "Thou hast no power except it be given thee from above." What stinging words! How Pilate cowered and tried then to reverse his verdict.

How often have little men with shriveled and withered souls, talked back to Christ, because they knew no better. When Pilate's eyes were opened ever so little, he labored to save Christ from the cross. He worked frantically and tried desperately, but to no avail. He then washed his hands in the presence of the mob, to signify his innocence in the matter. But did this help? It only *established beyond all doubt* his personal guilt, *for all time to come.* Pilate could have done differently if he would have. He could have refused to sentence Christ and taken the consequences, and been a man forever free and guiltless. But his desire for popularity won, and he is condemned to eternal guilt.

Christ is asking of millions today, "Why smitest thou me?" Think of the people who daily offend Christ by their sinful ways, make fun of His people, and work to destroy His cause. They are trying to smite Christ, for He said, "Inasmuch as ye do it unto one of these little ones which believe in me, ye do it unto me." One might as well smite Him personally as to try to turn one of His followers away from Him,

What a day when these shriveled, withered, puny moral and spiritual pigmys—these bits of "planetary eczema" in human form—come to stand in the whitening light of God's Judgment! Christ's eyes, burning with flames of eternal justice, will stare them down and burn their souls forever, as He asks them at last, *"Why smitest thou me?"*